LOUISE NEVELSON

AMERICAN WOMEN of ACHIEVEMENT

LOUISE NEVELSON

MICHAEL CAIN

CHELSEA HOUSE PUBLISHERS

NEW YORK • PHILADELPHIA

CHELSEA HOUSE PUBLISHERS
EDITOR-IN-CHIEF: Nancy Toff
EXECUTIVE EDITOR: Remmel T. Nunn
MANAGING EDITOR: Karyn Gullen Browne
COPY CHIEF: Juliann Barbato
PICTURE EDITOR: Adrian G. Allen
ART DIRECTOR: Maria Epes
MANUFACTURING MANAGER: Gerald Levine

American Women of Achievement
SENIOR EDITOR: Constance Jones

Staff for **LOUISE NEVELSON**
TEXT EDITOR: Marian W. Taylor
DEPUTY COPY CHIEF: Ellen Scordato
EDITORIAL ASSISTANT: Heather Lewis
PICTURE RESEARCHER: Emily Miller
ASSISTANT ART DIRECTOR: Loraine Machlin
DESIGN: Design Oasis
DESIGNER: Donna Sinisgalli
PRODUCTION COORDINATOR: Joseph Romano

Library of Congress Cataloging-in-Publication Data

Cain, Michael.
  Louise Nevelson.

  (American women of achievement)
  Bibliography: p.
  Includes index.
  Summary: Explores the life and artistry of the noted American
sculptor.
    1. Nevelson, Louise, 1900–   —Juvenile literature.
2. Sculptors—United States—Biography—Juvenile
literature. [1. Nevelson, Louise, 1900–1988.
2. Sculptors] I. Title. II. Series.
NB237.N43C35   1989   709′.2′4 [B] [92]   88-35261
ISBN 1-55546-671-0
      0-7910-0447-3 (pbk.)

CONTENTS

AMERICAN WOMEN of ACHIEVEMENT

Abigail Adams
women's rights advocate

Jane Addams
social worker

Louisa May Alcott
author

Marian Anderson
singer

Susan B. Anthony
woman suffragist

Ethel Barrymore
actress

Clara Barton
founder of the American Red Cross

Elizabeth Blackwell
physician

Nellie Bly
journalist

Margaret Bourke-White
photographer

Pearl Buck
author

Rachel Carson
biologist and author

Mary Cassatt
artist

Agnes De Mille
choreographer

Emily Dickinson
poet

Isadora Duncan
dancer

Amelia Earhart
aviator

Mary Baker Eddy
founder of the Christian Science church

Betty Friedan
feminist

Althea Gibson
tennis champion

Emma Goldman
political activist

Helen Hayes
actress

Lillian Hellman
playwright

Katharine Hepburn
actress

Karen Horney
psychoanalyst

Anne Hutchinson
religious leader

Mahalia Jackson
gospel singer

Helen Keller
humanitarian

Jeane Kirkpatrick
diplomat

Emma Lazarus
poet

Clare Boothe Luce
author and diplomat

Barbara McClintock
biologist

Margaret Mead
anthropologist

Edna St. Vincent Millay
poet

Julia Morgan
architect

Grandma Moses
painter

Louise Nevelson
sculptor

Sandra Day O'Connor
Supreme Court justice

Georgia O'Keeffe
painter

Eleanor Roosevelt
diplomat and humanitarian

Wilma Rudolph
champion athlete

Florence Sabin
medical researcher

Beverly Sills
opera singer

Gertrude Stein
author

Gloria Steinem
feminist

Harriet Beecher Stowe
author and abolitionist

Mae West
entertainer

Edith Wharton
author

Phillis Wheatley
poet

Babe Didrikson Zaharias
champion athlete

CHELSEA HOUSE PUBLISHERS

"Remember the Ladies"

MATINA S. HORNER

Remember the Ladies." That is what Abigail Adams wrote to her husband John, then a delegate to the Continental Congress, as the Founding Fathers met in Philadelphia to form a new nation in March of 1776. "Be more generous and favorable to them than your ancestors. Do not put such unlimited power in the hands of the Husbands. If particular care and attention is not paid to the Ladies," Abigail Adams warned, "we are determined to foment a Rebellion, and will not hold ourselves bound by any Laws in which we have no voice, or Representation."

The words of Abigail Adams, one of the earliest American advocates of women's rights, were prophetic. Because when we have not "remembered the ladies," they have, by their words and deeds, reminded us so forcefully of the omission that we cannot fail to remember them. For the history of American women is as interesting and varied as the history of our nation as a whole. American women have played an integral part in founding, settling, and building our country. Some we remember as remarkable women who—against great odds—achieved distinction in the public arena: Anne Hutchinson, who in the 17th century became a charismatic religious leader; Phillis Wheatley, an 18th-century black slave who became a poet; Susan B. Anthony, whose name is synonymous with the 19th-century women's rights movement, and who led the struggle to enfranchise women; and, in our own century, Amelia Earhart, the first woman to cross the Atlantic Ocean by air.

These extraordinary women certainly merit our admiration, but other women, "common women," many of them all but forgotten, should also be recognized for their contributions to American thought and culture. Women have been community builders; they have founded schools and formed voluntary associations to help those in need; they have assumed the major responsibility for rearing children, passing on from one generation to the next the values that keep a culture alive. These and innumerable other contributions, once ignored, are now being recognized by scholars, students, and the public. It is exciting and gratifying to realize that a part of our history that was hardly acknowledged a few generations ago is now being studied and brought to light.

In recent decades, the field of women's history has grown from obscurity to a politically controversial splinter movement to academic respectability, in many cases mainstreamed into such traditional disciplines as history, economics, and psychology. Scholars of women, both female and male, have organized research centers at such prestigious institutions as Wellesley College, Stanford University, and the University of California. Other notable centers for women's studies are the Center for the American Woman and Politics at the Eagleton Institute of Politics at Rutgers University; the Henry A. Murray Research Center for the Study of Lives, at Radcliffe College; and the Women's Research and Education Institute, the research arm of the Congressional Caucus on Women's Issues. Other scholars and public figures have established archives and libraries, such as the Schlesinger Library on the History of Women in America, at Radcliffe College, and the Sophia Smith Collection, at Smith College, to collect and preserve the written and tangible legacies of women.

From the initial donation of the Women's Rights Collection in 1943, the Schlesinger Library grew to encompass vast collections documenting the manifold accomplishments of American women. Simultaneously, the women's movement in general and the academic discipline of women's studies in particular also began with a narrow definition and gradually expanded their mandate. Early causes such as woman suffrage and social reform, abolition and organized labor were joined by newer concerns such as the history of women in business and the professions and in politics and government; the study of the family; and social issues such as health policy and education.

Women, as historian Arthur M. Schlesinger, jr., once pointed out, "have constituted the most spectacular casualty of traditional history. They have made up at least half the human race, but you could never tell that by looking at the books historians write." The new breed of historians is remedying that omission. They have written books about immigrant women and about working-class women who struggled for survival in cities and about black women who met the challenges of life in rural areas. They are telling the stories of women who, despite the barriers of tradition and economics, became lawyers and doctors and public figures.

The women's studies movement has also led scholars to question traditional interpretations of their respective disciplines. For example, the study of war has traditionally been an exercise in military and political analysis, an examination of strategies planned and executed by men. But scholars of women's history have pointed out that wars have also been periods of tremendous change and even opportunity for women, because the very absence of men on the home front enabled them to expand their educational, economic, and professional activities and to assume leadership in their homes.

The early scholars of women's history showed a unique brand of courage in choosing to investigate new subjects and take new approaches to old ones. Often, like their subjects, they endured criticism and even ostracism by their academic colleagues. But their efforts have unquestionably been worthwhile, because with the publication of each new study and book another piece of the historical patchwork is sewn into place, revealing an increasingly comprehensive picture of the role of women in our rich and varied history.

Such books on groups of women are essential, but books that focus on the lives of individuals are equally indispensable. Biographies can be inspirational, offering their readers the example of people with vision who have looked outside themselves for their goals and have often struggled against great obstacles to achieve them. Marian Anderson, for instance, had to overcome racial bigotry in order to perfect her art and perform as a concert singer. Isadora Duncan defied the rules of classical dance to find true artistic freedom. Jane Addams had to break down society's notions of the proper role for women in order to create new social institutions, notably the settlement house. All of these women had to come to terms both with themselves and with the world in which they lived. Only then could they move ahead as pioneers in their chosen callings.

Biography can inspire not only by adulation but also by realism. It helps us to see not only the qualities in others that we hope to emulate, but also, perhaps, the weaknesses that made them "human." By helping us identify with the subject on a more personal level they help us to feel that we, too, can achieve such goals. We read about Eleanor Roosevelt, for instance, who occupied a unique and seemingly enviable position as the wife of the president. Yet we can sympathize with her inner dilemma: an inherently shy woman, she had to force herself to live a most public life in order to use her position to benefit others. We may not be able to imagine ourselves having the immense poetic talent of Emily Dickinson, but from her story we can understand the challenges faced by a creative woman who was expected to fulfill many family responsibilities. And though few of us will ever reach the level of athletic accomplishment displayed by Wilma Rudolph or Babe Zaharias, we can still appreciate their spirit, their overwhelming will to excel.

A biography is a multifaceted lens. It is first of all a magnification, the intimate examination of one particular life. But at the same time, it is a wide-angle lens, informing us about the world in which the subject lived. We come away from reading about one life knowing more about the social, political, and economic fabric of the time. It is for this reason, perhaps, that the great New England essayist Ralph Waldo Emerson wrote, in 1841, "There is properly no history: only biography." And it is also why biography, and particularly women's biography, will continue to fascinate writers and readers alike.

Sculptor Louise Nevelson (seen here in 1956) practiced her art for more than 30 years before she received her first major museum exhibition.

ONE

Dawn's Wedding Feast

Late one December afternoon, a delivery truck eased up to the curb of a mid-Manhattan street. Workers quickly unloaded the vehicle and carried its contents into a nearby building. Waiting inside were four people who began to unpack the shipment: an assortment of bulky, strangely shaped wooden objects. The year was 1959; the building was the Museum of Modern Art; the objects were sculptures that would rock the art world.

Sculptor Louise Nevelson had prepared for this day with three months of hard labor. Barely pausing to eat, sleeping in her clothes when she was exhausted, she had worked frantically, sawing, hammering, arranging, and painting. The result was *Dawn's Wedding Feast*, a group of sculptures composed of wooden columns, boxes, disks, chair legs, picture frames, and fragments of scrap lumber, all of them painted white. Planning to surprise the public with this unique, all-white environment, she had worked secretly, telling only a handful of associates about her scheme. In order to avoid attention, she had picked dusk to have the sculptures brought from her studio to the museum.

Sixteen Americans, a major show of contemporary American artists, was to open at the Museum of Modern Art on December 16. Nevelson, then 60, had spent decades struggling for recognition. Since the 1930s, she had gradually built a reputation in the art world, displaying her work at various galleries and often receiving favorable reviews from art critics. But she had never before been offered a major museum exhibition, which would confirm her position as a leading artist. And, al-

13

though the art world had admired her sculptures, few members of the general public—particularly the art-buying public—knew of her or her dazzling work.

"For 40 years I wanted to jump out of windows," Nevelson said years later, describing the frustrating decades before her art finally emerged from obscurity. But she also recalled that she had never wavered in her determination to succeed as an artist. "No one could move me till I got what I wanted," she told Diana MacKown, her longtime friend and assistant. (MacKown recorded the comment in *Dawns + Dusks*, a remarkable book composed in 1976 from taped conversations with Nevelson.)

As soon as the pieces for her show were delivered, Nevelson and her helpers began to set them up. On one side of the exhibition room, the sculptor placed *Dawn's Wedding Chapel*, a 16-foot-long wall of white-painted boxes stacked on top of one another. The boxes were filled with what one critic would describe as "newels, finials, slats, knobs, dowels, mitered corners, lintels, studs, and maybe an old croquet set." Other pieces included *Dawn's Wedding Mirror* (a large box

Ornate columns dominate Dawn's Wedding Feast, *Nevelson's white sculpture of 1959. One art critic called the work "bizarre, humorous, and resplendent."*

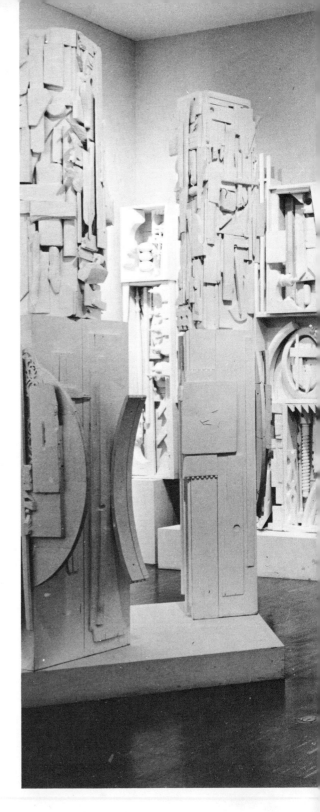

Nevelson said officials of the Museum of Modern Art (above) took her "by storm and surprise" when they invited her to take part in 1959's Sixteen Americans *show.*

that contained a toilet seat framed by a wooden oval), *Dawn's Wedding Pillow* (a set of boxes arranged to form steps), and several tall, thin columns encrusted with white wooden objects. Two slender pillars hung from the ceiling; at the center of the room stood a pair of massive columns representing a bride and groom. In *Dawn's Wedding*

Feast, Nevelson had created a whole new world, a place both mysterious and beautiful.

Viewers were stunned by the *Wedding Feast*. "The air is electric," exclaimed one museum official at the opening. Describing Nevelson's "extraordinary white room," art critic Dore Ashton called it "bizarre, humorous, and at the same time, resplendent." The show imparted "an overwhelming feeling of cathedral silence and calm," said the *New Yorker* magazine. And *Art News* magazine observed that "a whole environment has succumbed to an artist's iron will and velvet eyes."

Nevelson's work soon attracted serious art collectors. Millionaire Nelson Rockefeller, governor of New York State at the time, bought several pieces from the *Wedding Feast* exhibition, and the Museum of Modern Art itself acquired two of the show's white pillars for its permanent collection. Nevelson was delighted with the sales, but she wished the environment could have remained intact. "If any museum would have just been interested," she said later, "I'd have given it to them." After some parts of the *Wedding Feast* were sold individually, Nevelson dismantled the rest to use in other sculptures.

At 60, Louise Nevelson was finally recognized as one of the most important artists in America. But she was philosophical about her triumph. "It is

Nevelson (left) and her friend Diana MacKown share a quiet moment in 1986.
A decade earlier, the two had collaborated on Nevelson's memoirs, Dawns + Dusks.

as hard to take success as it is failure," she told MacKown later. "Being a public person requires a lot of things. Above all, self-protection. You have to know how to handle it. However," she added, "it was only after I was established that I didn't feel the need to pound my head against the wall."

17

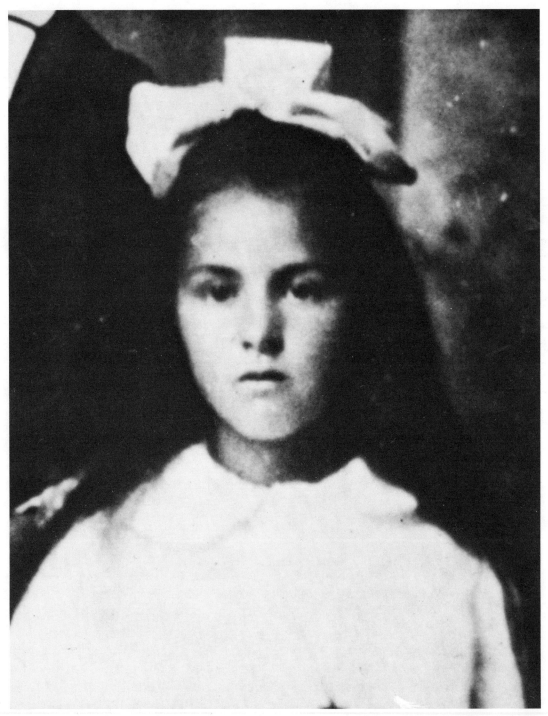

Louise Berliawsky, seen here at the age of seven, was only three when her father sailed for America. After he left, she stopped speaking for six months.

TWO

Outsider

Born in Kiev, Russia, on September 23, 1899, Louise Berliawsky was the second child of Minna Berliawsky and her husband, Isaac, a lumber merchant. Berliawsky made a good living, but because he was Jewish, he found his business opportunities limited. Russia had a long history of anti-Semitism (hatred of Jews), and its laws prohibited Jews from owning land. Not allowed to raise their own timber, Berliawsky and other Jewish lumber sellers had to buy their wood from gentile landowners, often at inflated prices.

Economic restrictions, however, were not the worst troubles confronted by Russia's Jews. Far more fearsome were the *pogroms* (organized massacres) that periodically swept the nation's Jewish communities. In 1881, 18 years before Louise's birth, a violent mob attacked Kiev's Jews, killing and

beating innocent people, destroying synagogues, and burning Jewish homes and shops. In the wake of this terrifying assault, many of Isaac Berliawsky's relatives had emigrated to the United States. Berliawsky had wanted to join them, but he had felt obliged to stay with his aging parents.

On a timber-buying trip in 1895, Berliawsky visited Shushneky, a tiny village on the Dnieper River. There he met and fell in love with Minna Smolerank, the beautiful 16-year-old daughter of a village farmer. He soon asked her to be his wife, but she was reluctant. Although Berliawsky, tall and slim, with dark hair and blue eyes, was very attractive, Minna Smolerank had hoped to marry someone who would settle in her hometown. But Berliawsky was persistent, and she finally relented. After their wedding, the young couple settled in Kiev, where, in 1897, their first child, Nathan, was born. Louise arrived two years later, and Anita in 1902.

Berliawsky had never given up his dream of moving to America. There, he thought, a Jew could earn a decent living and raise a family in security and peace. When his father died in 1902, he decided the time had come. He left for the United States, promising to send for his wife, children, and mother as soon as he had established himself. Three-year-old Louise was deeply upset by her father's departure. Unconsciously protesting what she must have regarded as abandonment, she stopped speaking entirely. Six months passed before the little girl, much to her mother's relief, regained her ability to talk.

When Isaac Berliawsky left for America, his wife and children went to live with the Smoleranks in Shushneky. The reunion delighted Minna Berliawsky, who had missed her family and her native village terribly. She was heartbroken when, two years later, her husband summoned her and the children, along with his mother, to Rockland, Maine. Minna knew she would never see her own parents again. Her sorrow over leaving them never truly healed.

Louise was almost six years old when she left Russia for her new life in America. For as long as she could remember, she had lived in a tiny village, surrounded by a tightly knit circle of relatives and family friends. Now she was traveling across the world to a land where no one knew

Battered survivors of a pogrom assemble in a village near Kiev. Pogroms—violent mob attacks on Jews—occurred with tragic frequency in 19th-century Russia.

Trolley tracks bisect Main Street in Rockland, seen here at about the time Louise Berliawsky and her family settled in the Maine seacost town.

her, no one spoke her language. The journey from Shushneky to Rockland, made by horse cart, train, and steamship, took several months.

When the U.S.-bound steamer stopped in Liverpool, England, Minna Berliawsky took her children to a candy store, the first they had ever seen. Louise was entranced. Wide-eyed, she gazed at the rows of sparkling glass containers, each brimming with brightly colored hard candies. "It looked like heaven," she recalled later. This vision would continue to excite her. Its afterimage—shelves lined with containers full of intriguing objects—would appear in some of her greatest sculpture.

After his wife, children, and mother arrived in Rockland, Isaac Berliawsky installed them in a house overlooking the city's busy waterfront. Now in his

A 1905 crayon drawing—Louise Berliawsky's first self-portrait—shows a smiling six-year-old waiting for supper in her Rockland, Maine, home.

middle thirties, he was slowly establishing himself in the lumber and contracting business. In only a few years, he was to become one of the region's most active businessmen, buying and selling land and lumber, building and selling houses.

The Berliawsky family, one of the handful of Jewish families in Rockland, soon learned to speak English, but that was not enough to make them fit into local social circles. Populated chiefly by conservative Protestant New En-

glanders, Rockland did not readily accept foreigners, especially Jews. The Berliawsky children's feelings of isolation were increased by their mother's insistence on wearing stylish European clothing. "When my mother walked downtown in Rockland, everybody stopped to watch her," recalled Louise Nevelson years later. "She also dressed us in very expensive clothes—fancier than I found comfortable for Rockland."

Isaac Berliawsky quickly learned the

ways of American commerce, but his wife had trouble adjusting to her new life. Yearning for the family and homeland she had left behind, she felt like a stranger in Rockland. Unlike her husband, she had no circle of friendly business associates, and she had little in common with her Christian neighbors, whose social life revolved around their church activities.

Lonely and dispirited, Minna Berliawsky was afflicted by frequent bouts of uncontrollable weeping and severe headaches. "She'd get into bed and stay for several weeks at a time," her daughter wrote later. "There was noth-

Minna Berliawsky stands behind her husband and children in this 1906 family portrait. From left to right are Anita, Nathan, Isaac (holding Lillian), and Louise.

ing we could do.... I never saw her happy."

Nevertheless, Louise and her siblings (including Lillian, who was born in Rockland in 1906) grew up with strong family attachments. Speaking to her friend and biographer, Arnold Glimcher, many years later, Louise Nevelson said, "I adored my parents. My mother was freethinking and had strong socialist ideas. My father believed in equal rights for women, and I remember everyone said that he was a business genius—but he was just too busy and I didn't see enough of him."

Isaac Berliawsky loved music, a taste he passed on to his children. He was one of the first residents of Rockland to acquire a newfangled Victrola (a record player with a long, curved horn), and he owned a fine collection of opera recordings. Pleased by his children's interest in music, he bought them a piano and provided them with violin, piano, and voice lessons. The girls enjoyed playing and singing and often staged musical performances for the household.

Berliawsky, who also loved antiques, became an avid collector. Here again, he was emulated by his children, Louise in particular. In Rockland, she combed the beaches, looking for interesting stones and bits of driftwood,

Ninth graders line up for a 1913 portrait in Rockland, Maine. Russian-born Louise Berliawsky (fifth from left) later said she felt like an "outsider" in school.

which she would store in little boxes in her room. This practice gave another hint of the future: In years to come, she would base much of her work on the "found objects" she gathered on roadsides and city streets.

Louise thought her father was "a piece of genius," but his unpredictable behavior and sudden bursts of rage made him difficult to live with. "He was too hard for me," his daughter said in her memoirs. "When he came home, it was like an engine. I always felt it was like a furnace downstairs going chuga-chuga-chug. So we didn't communicate much." The two did manage to communicate, however, on the subject of Berliawsky's occupation, which fascinated his daughter. She listened attentively when he talked about woodworking, and she watched carefully as he supervised the construction of a new house for his family.

The Berliawskys' house was about a mile from the Rockland public school. Louise and her siblings, who all came home for lunch, walked back and forth twice a day. Louise found most of her classes dull; a slow reader, she received mediocre grades. From the beginning, however, she excelled at art. In the second grade, she drew a picture of a sunflower, showing it as a huge ball fringed with miniature petals. The drawing was praised as "original" by her art teacher. "I didn't know what original meant," she recalled later, "but it made me feel very good."

Always intrigued by wooden furniture, Louise Berliawsky made this pen-and-ink drawing of an antique chair when she was 17 years old.

The art teacher visited the Rockland school once a week, but Louise drew and painted every day. "When I was a baby I knew that I was going to be an artist," she told Arnold Glimcher. "As long as I wasn't so smart, I was going to be great! What else could I do?" By the time she was seven she had made up her mind to become a sculptor. She even felt a physical comfort in the presence of art; during the icy Maine winters, the art room seemed to her the warmest place in the school. "I'm sure it didn't have more heat," she recalled, "but it always seemed to be warmer. I couldn't wait to get to that room."

For Louise, art was not confined to pictures and sculpture. She was very fond of hats, and when she was 14 she decided to paint one. Cutting out a stencil in the shape of a butterfly, she carefully reproduced it all over a piece of linen. She attached the painted fabric to a hat frame and proudly wore it to school every day for weeks. Louise Nevelson never outgrew her passion for hats. As an adult, in fact, her extravagant headgear prompted admirers to give her an affectionate nickname: the Hat.

By the time she was a teenager, Louise was concentrating almost exclusively on dancing, piano lessons, and art classes. Her parents were supportive, even when she neglected her other studies. They both assured her that a person's sex had nothing to do with talent, that it was one's ability that counted. She never felt, she recalled, that "being a female was any handicap."

In high school, she was elected captain of the girls' basketball team and vice-president of the glee club. Still, she never felt she was part of the school's social life. She later told her friend Diana MacKown, "Rockland was a WASP [white Anglo-Saxon Protestant] Yankee town, and look, an immigrant family pays a price. Even if you were Jesus Christ Superstar, you were still an outsider."

In her 1984 biography of Nevelson, *Breaking Tradition*, Natalie Bober suggests that anti-Semitism was responsible for the young woman's sense of isolation. She offers an anecdote to illustrate this argument. "One day," she reports, "standing at her locker after basketball practice, Louise overheard some of the team members talking about the upcoming dance on the following Saturday night. As they talked about which boy would escort each girl, Louise heard the captain of the boys' team say, 'Do I have to take that Jew?' "

In April 1917, two months before Louise graduated from high school, the United States entered World War I, the European conflict that had been raging since 1914. Louise was not directly affected by the war, but it set in motion a chain of events that would change her life. In 1917, the U.S. Navy had only a few warships. To provide security for American troopships crossing the Atlantic, the government began to lease and arm civilian merchant ships, many of which were refitted at Rockland's shipyards.

Under repair at the Maine port in 1917 was a vessel owned by four Russian-born brothers named Nevelson. When Bernard Nevelson, the oldest brother, arrived in Rockland to check on the ship, he visited the law office where high school senior Louise

Berliawsky was working as a part-time secretary. Realizing that Nevelson was Jewish, she spoke to him in Yiddish.

Nevelson was charmed by the young woman, and when he returned to his New York office, he told his younger brother Charles about her. A few weeks later, Charles Nevelson arrived in Rockland, telephoned Louise, and asked her to have dinner with him. Before she even met him, she later told Diana MacKown, she knew what he would do next: "I took my mother into the kitchen and I said, 'Mr. Nevelson is here, and he's going to propose to me this evening and I'm accepting.'"

Louise told her mother she "was not going to be married and lead a conventional life"; she was "going to be an artist." "Bewitched and bewildered" by her daughter's plans, Minna Berliawsky said, "You know, it's going to be a hard life, being an artist, to live that way." Louise responded, "It isn't how you live, it's how you finish." She had been correct about Charles Nevelson's intentions: He soon asked her to marry him. "I explained very carefully," she recalled, "that I wanted to study art, that I was going to pursue a creative life, and he said that was all right and there was no reason I couldn't continue. We could still get married." Then she told him she did not want to have children, at least not soon. He had no objections.

Charles Nevelson was 15 years older than Louise Berliawsky and consider-

Louise Berliawsky, seen here on a Rockland, Maine, street in 1919, described herself as a person with "big arms and big legs."

Shipowner Charles Nevelson, 15 years older than Louise Berliawsky, proposed to her soon after their first date. The couple married in 1920.

ably shorter. Describing herself at this age, she later wrote, "I weighed about what I do now, and I had big arms and big legs. They weren't out of proportion, but they were biggish. (I'm five feet, seven and a half inches.) And I related myself to the wonderful neo-classic colonial houses in Maine. . . . I felt that I was related, that my arms and legs related to those columns."

Older and shorter he may have been, but Nevelson was sophisticated. He was from New York, and he was a Russian Jew; Louise had more in common with him than with the young men of her own age in Rockland. She accepted his proposal. Several months

later, Nevelson invited Louise and Minna Berliawsky to visit New York City and meet the rest of his family.

It was Louise's first trip to the great metropolis. "I suppose I was a little afraid of New York City," she recalled later. Soon, however, she felt at home. "You know," she observed in *Dawns + Dusks*, "they talk about the dirt in New York. Well, for me, it's so opulent, rich. It's the richest city in the world. I love the architecture, all those big, mountainous buildings." Louise Berliawsky could not know it at the time, but she would one day put her own mark on the city, which was to be her home for the rest of her long life.

Enchanted by such "mountainous" Manhattan structures as the Flatiron Building (above, center), Louise Berliawsky defined New York City as a "great big sculpture."

Young Mrs. Charles Nevelson was delighted to settle in Manhattan, but she found her husband's family oppressively "shallow."

THREE

Marriage

On June 12, 1920, Louise Berliawsky, not quite 21 years old, married 36-year-old Charles Nevelson. They picked Boston, midway between Maine and New York, as the site for their traditional Jewish wedding. After honeymooning in New Orleans and Havana, Cuba, the couple settled in Manhattan. In the 1920s the United States was in the midst of a great economic boom, and New York, with its stock exchange and fast-growing banks and businesses, was at the center of it. The city teemed with recent immigrants from many nations; new buildings were being constructed everywhere; the arts—painting, sculpture, music, theater—flourished.

Louise Nevelson reveled in the variety of New York's inhabitants, in its graceful mansions and tall buildings, and, most of all, in its glittering cultural life. Her husband supported her desire to study the arts, and she began right away, enrolling in acting classes and singing lessons.

For the most part, Nevelson enjoyed herself. She was studying the arts in New York and she was married to a wealthy man who placed no serious restraints on her freedom. She did not, however, enjoy socializing with the Nevelson family's friends. Like the Nevelsons themselves, most of their associates were wealthy Russian emigrés. They were well educated and cultured, but to Louise Nevelson they seemed shallow, concerned more with the surface than with the real substance of life. "They thought they were terribly refined," she wrote later. "Within their circle you could know Beethoven, but God forbid if you *were* Beethoven. You were not allowed to be a creator, you

Fashionable New Yorkers enjoy an evening out during the 1920s. Accustomed to quiet Rockland, Maine, Louise Nevelson was dazzled by Manhattan's glittering nightlife.

were just supposed to be an audience."

To a young woman who intended to become a great artist, such an atmosphere was chilling. Still, Nevelson's first years in New York were full of hope and pleasure. With her sister Anita, who often visited her, she made the rounds of art galleries, museums, concerts, and plays. She and her husband, she recalled, "had decided not to have children and that I was just to continue my studies." She was in the midst of the life she had longed for.

In 1921, however, she realized she was pregnant. Myron (Mike) Nevelson was born on February 23, 1922. Soon afterward, his mother later wrote, "I went into a depression, right down to the tip of my toe." Nevelson loved her baby, but she was overwhelmed by the thought of being responsible for another human life. How could she care for a child and become an artist at the same time? "Here I had a son," she wrote later, "and I didn't feel like living. I just felt like I was lost."

To make matters worse, Charles

Nevelson began to study at the Art Students League (above) at the suggestion of Anita Berliawsky, who hoped art lessons would raise her sister's low spirits.

The works of Pablo Picasso (seen here in a 1907 self-portrait) profoundly impressed Nevelson, who said the Spanish-born artist "defined the structure of the world."

Nevelson decided that little Mike should grow up in a more rural setting. In 1924, when the boy was two, the family moved to the New York City suburb of Mount Vernon. Here, Louise Nevelson felt completely cut off from the art world she longed to join. Her gloomy mood was lightened by the arrival of Anita Berliawsky, who moved in to help take care of Mike. Anita encouraged her sister to sign up for Saturday drawing classes at the Art Students League in New York City. With these classes, Nevelson began a slow reentry into her art studies, and by 1926 she was taking private painting lessons in addition to her drawing class.

At this time Nevelson was equally interested in all the arts, from painting and sculpture to theater and music. "I had a long-range view of my life," she wrote in her memoirs. "I was branching out and reaching out in many directions.... If I was going to say what I knew I wanted to say, I had to know ... just how to say it. [I understood] that all of these arts were pretty much one. All of them were essential; one supported the other."

As Louise Nevelson spent more and more time studying art, dancing, and singing, Charles Nevelson became increasingly resentful. Louise Nevelson had never felt comfortable in the role of traditional wife, and her husband's attitude both puzzled and annoyed

her. "He expected me home at 7:30 for dinner," she recalled later. "But what do we have a maid for," she asked him, "if not to get your dinner?" Writing about this dialogue, biographer Natalie Bober observes, "It probably never occurred to her that Charles might have wanted her home for dinner simply because he enjoyed being with her. He wanted a wife. She wanted art."

In 1926, Louise Nevelson encountered a new world of art. "I saw the first Picassos," she recalled, "and it gave me a definition of structure of the world and every object in the world." Pablo Picasso, now recognized as one of the greatest artists of the 20th century, was then a revolutionary modern artist especially noted for his cubist paintings.

Rather than showing their subjects as they appeared to the naked eye, cubists broke them into their geometric equivalents. These artists presented natural forms—human beings, animals, still lifes—as masses of cubelike shapes. A cubist painter would show all sides of a person or an object at the same time, as in the Picasso portraits that include both their subjects' profiles and full-face likenesses.

Nevelson was wildly excited by her discovery of *l'art moderne* (modern art). "Without Picasso giving us the cube, I would not have freed myself for my own work," she said later. "Picasso changed our thinking and he gave us structure. Of course, when you recognize that, you can vary it. But that is your foundation."

Soon after she discovered Picasso, Nevelson enrolled in the newly established Theatre Arts Institute in Brooklyn, New York. At the same time, financial setbacks forced Charles Nevelson to sell the Mount Vernon house and move his family to Brooklyn. This was convenient for his wife, because she would now be close to the school where she was studying. As always, the Berliawsky sisters remained close. Anita, who had married, moved to Brooklyn with her husband. Lillian, now 20 years old, settled in with the Nevelsons and took a teaching job at the private kindergarten where Mike was a pupil.

Charles Nevelson was still a wealthy man, but his financial situation continued to worsen. In 1929, he decided to move once more, this time to an apartment on Manhattan's East 91st Street. Louise Nevelson dropped out of the Theatre Arts Institute and took Mike out of private school. After the series of moves and the apparent dead end of her career as an artist, she again became profoundly depressed. At 29, she felt she had lost sight of her goals. Decades later she described her condition at the time. It was, she said, "like a trance. . . . You're so unhappy that you get frozen and you don't even know you're unhappy. And I saw no way of breaking this state of mind."

Nevelson's dark state of mind, however, soon brightened. Walking disconsolately along New York's Fifth Avenue one winter day in 1929, she wandered into the Metropolitan Museum of Art. There she saw a display of Japanese theater robes, a sight that instantly elevated her spirits and helped shape her development as an artist.

The costumes were intricately woven from gold thread and adorned with gold medallions. "Each robe was a universe in itself," Nevelson recalled in *Dawns + Dusks*. "I looked and I sat down without thinking and I had a barrel of tears on the right eye and a barrel of tears on the left eye . . . and then my nose was running . . . and I wanted to go to the bathroom. Everything was open. And then I knew and I said, oh, my God, life is worth living. . . . And so I sat there and sat and wept and wept and sat. . . . I went home and it gave me a whole new life."

Nevelson began studying again with a passion. She enrolled full-time in drawing classes at the Art Students League, where the principal topic of discussion was *l'art moderne*. Many of the League's teachers were first-rate artists as well as instructors, but none taught the techniques used by such avant-garde artists as Picasso and Matisse. What Nevelson wanted, she said, was "to be of the present time instead of the past." How could she find out what she needed to know? Her fellow students at the Art Students League insisted there was only one teacher

Ruined by the stock market collapse of 1929, an investor tries to raise money. Charles Nevelson's finances were shaken by the crash, but he remained solvent.

who could explain the cubists and their work. His name was Hans Hofmann, and his school was in Munich, Germany.

But Charles Nevelson, already distressed by the amount of time his wife was devoting to her art studies in New York, did not approve of her taking a trip to Europe. The Nevelson marriage was now showing signs of serious stress. Charles insisted that Louise pay more attention to her duties as a wife and mother and start acting like a "normal" New York matron. Now that she was really getting a taste of a life in

the arts, however, she was more determined than ever not to be held back.

"I had recognized from the beginning that truly I didn't have much in common with my husband," Nevelson recalled later. "I was never married in the true soul sense." Now, in the absence of any romantic bond, the frustrations of married life were growing intolerable; the relationship that had helped to free her from Rockland had turned into what she called a "sort of imprisonment."

In her characteristically uninhibited style, Nevelson later talked to Diana

MacKown about this period in her life. "I saw in the paper that this girl was on trial, because she wanted to go to a party and her husband aggravated her, and he was sitting on the windowsill and she threw him out," she said. "Gave him a little push. And I thought, there but for the grace of God go I. And then I thought, I can't stay here because I'll do something desperate. I must get out of this."

In 1931, Nevelson took Mike, then nine years old, to visit her family in Maine. There, she discussed her future

Staying in Maine while his mother attends art classes in Germany, nine-year-old Mike Nevelson relaxes on his grandmother's backyard swing.

Nevelson, who was intrigued by such modern European paintings as Henri Matisse's Liseuse Sur Fond Noir *(above), made up her mind to study abroad in 1931.*

with her mother, who was ill but as sympathetic as ever. Nevelson talked about her intense desire to go to Germany to study with Hans Hofmann but said that because her mother was not well, she hesitated to make the trip. She recorded the subsequent conversation in her memoirs.

"As ill as she was, she said, 'Louise, you must go. You always wanted to continue in your art. If I don't survive, it will make no difference. You go and study. We'll send you an allowance, and we'll take care of Mike and see that he has everything he needs.' Then she added, 'Look, you don't have to stay married. Before that, you were so vital.' " Her mother's words reinforced Nevelson's convictions. "She sensed it," Nevelson said. "I was crippled up, and I knew what it was. If you have got a living force and you're not using it, nature kicks you back. The blood boils just like you put it in a pot." Her mother, she added, "was the one who really gave me the courage to take my freedom."

Nevelson was determined to go to Germany no matter what her husband thought. Still, she was depressed by the failure of her marriage. "Everything had collapsed and it was of my own choosing in a way, but that didn't make it easier," she recalled later. More painful still was cutting herself off, even temporarily, from her son and her family. "The weight of leaving Mike was a great responsibility," she wrote years afterward. "The guilts of motherhood were the worst guilts in the world for me. They were really insurmountable."

Nevelson knew she had to "claim [her] own life." But, she said later, "I don't think I realized the price that would be demanded for what I wanted. I've been so lonely for long periods of my life that if a rat walked in, I would have welcomed it." But she had made her decision; in the winter of 1931 she set sail for Europe.

Louise Nevelson (above), was 31 and full of high hopes when she entered Hans Hofmann's drawing class, but her lessons with the German artist proved disappointing.

FOUR

Searching for Forms

In the 1930s, a rising tide of German nationalism and economic discontent was sweeping Nazi leader Adolf Hitler into power. The Nazis practiced a particularly vicious form of anti-Semitism, which would eventually result in the systematic murder of 6 million European Jews. By 1931, signs of the impending Holocaust had become plainly visible: Hitler had spelled out his plan for destroying the Jewish people in his best-selling autobiography, *Mein Kampf* (My Struggle), and the Nazi party had come in second in the national elections.

Determined to study with Hans Hofmann in Germany, Louise Nevelson ignored this gathering storm. As it turned out, however, her experience with Hofmann failed to justify the risk. He allowed her to enroll in his drawing class, but he paid her little attention.

Nevelson later realized that Hofmann, who was Jewish, was far more interested in getting out of Germany than in teaching his students. "I don't blame him for that," she said afterward, "but I had made my own sacrifice to come and I was disappointed."

Under pressure from the Nazis, Hofmann closed his school and left Germany three months after Nevelson's arrival. Hoping to gain something from her trip, she stayed on in Munich, where she had met a number of artists and actors. Through them, she got a few jobs as a movie extra. She enjoyed the atmosphere of the film world, but acting, she decided, was not for her. Using the money she had earned from her film roles, she traveled through northern Italy, where she saw some of the magnificent art of the Renaissance, then went to Paris for a short stay.

Painter and teacher Hans Hofmann (above) sailed for America soon after Nevelson arrived in Munich. A year later, she enrolled in his art class in New York.

She was enthralled by the great museums in the French capital, but she was filled with self-doubt and guilt about leaving her son. His letters both amused her and touched her deeply. Once, when she had sent him a picture of herself, he wrote back, "I received your photograph. Grandma thinks you look crazy, but she's old and don't know much. I think you look good just like a great artist."

"I think people should think a million times before they give birth," Nevelson wrote later. "You are depriving another human being of so many things. . . . That struggle blinds you.

That's the price, the great price." In Paris, she started writing poetry, a practice she would continue for the rest of her life. A stanza from a poem called "Paris 1931" suggests her feelings about her marriage and her son:

My child, why did it have to be
So that we together be in such mystery
to each other.
Was it your father? . . .
When you are older do not scold her.

Back in Maine at the end of 1931, Nevelson was relieved to find her mother fully recovered and her son thriving. Mike got along very well with his grandfather and his uncle Nathan, who were teaching him carpentry and woodworking. Satisfied that all was well in Rockland, Nevelson returned to New York. There she reentered the Art Students League and settled down to paint, draw, and sculpt. But she was still restless, and in the summer of 1932, she decided to go back to Paris. Charles Nevelson had given her a diamond bracelet when Mike was born; now she pawned it to pay for her trip abroad.

This time she stayed only a few weeks, studying the cathedrals, museums, and art galleries. She especially liked the Musée de l'Homme, a Paris museum that exhibited cultural objects from around the world. Here she viewed the primitive African masks and sculptures that had inspired some of Picasso's paintings. "I went in and saw, not only the masks, I saw an

German leader Adolf Hitler salutes a cheering crowd in the early 1930s. Hitler's increasingly powerful Nazi party posed a deadly threat to Germany's Jews.

animal, and recognized the *energy*. And I think that was a milestone," she wrote. "It's true that Picasso had already found African sculpture, but until I went there I had never seen it. I recognized the lines and the strength and the power."

When she returned to New York in the fall of 1932, she faced her situation. "I was altogether on my own, and I knew that I would just have to swim or sink," she later told biographer Diana MacKown. "No one was going to swim for me and no one was going to sink for me." She and her husband agreed that their marriage was over. Although

they would not be formally divorced for another 10 years, they never tried to reconcile. They would, however, stay in touch to discuss the upbringing of their son.

Hans Hofmann, who had emigrated to the United States, was now teaching at the Art Students League, and Nevelson signed up to study with him. This time around, he paid more attention to her work. "Once in class at the League," she recalled later, "he picked up one of my abstract figures and said to the class, 'You see this, this is bigger than life.' I had more friends after that day!"

Nevelson was fascinated by Hofmann's interpretation of the cubist movement, which she called "one of the greatest awarenesses that the human mind has ever come to." He defined it, she recalled, as "the push and pull. Positive and negative. Cubism gives you a *block* of space for light. A *block* of space for shadow. Light and shade are in the universe, but the cube ... translates nature into a structure." In later years, Nevelson freely conceded that all her work was "stamped" by cubism.

Also studying at the League was Marjorie Eaton, a young Californian who shared Nevelson's enthusiasm for the arts. The two women, who liked each other immediately, decided to rent an apartment together. In 1933, Eaton introduced Nevelson to the celebrated Mexican artist Diego Rivera. Rivera had come to New York City to create a monumental mural in Rockefeller Center as well as smaller paintings in two Manhattan schools. He needed assistants for this work, and he asked Nevelson and Eaton to join him.

The young women soon moved into the building where Rivera and his wife, Frida Kahlo, lived and worked. During the day Nevelson mixed paint and applied color washes to the walls Rivera planned to paint; in the evening she and Eaton socialized with Rivera, Kahlo, and their friends. Nevelson was enchanted by her new associates. "There was grandeur there," she said, speaking of Rivera. "As a human being and as a creative man, he was a great artist." And she admired Kahlo, herself a well-known painter, for her direct approach to her goals: "She knew what she wanted in life and she was living that life." Everyone was welcome at the artists' apartment. "I was never in a home like Diego's," said Nevelson. "Princesses and queens ... one lady richer than God. And workmen, laborers. He made no distinction, and all were treated like one body of people."

Nevelson was intrigued by Rivera's use of primitive Mexican Indian art forms, which reminded her of the works of the Pemaquid Indians near Rockland and of the African sculptures at the Musée de l'Homme. She did not, however, much care for the *fresco* technique (painting on fresh plaster) Rivera used, and she was not interested in doing the research required for his historical and social-commentary works. One of these, a colossal mural entitled *Man at the Crossroads*, stirred up a hornet's nest.

The mural had been commissioned by conservative millionaire Nelson Rockefeller; it was to embellish the Manhattan commercial center that bore his family's name. Rockefeller, grandson of industrialist John D. Rockefeller, knew Rivera was an avowed Communist. Perhaps he should not have been surprised when the artist added a likeness of Russian Communist leader Vladimir Lenin to the mural.

Artist Diego Rivera stands in front of one of his Mexico City paintings in the 1930s. He and his wife, painter Frida Kahlo, became Nevelson's close friends.

Re-created in Mexico City, Rivera's controversial mural Man at the Crossroads *includes a portrait of Communist leader Leon Trotsky (center, with beard).*

But Rockefeller was not only astonished, he was outraged.

He demanded the removal of Lenin's portrait. Rivera refused. In the end, Rockefeller destroyed the mural, although he paid Rivera his full $21,000 fee. The artist gave it all away. "People would know when he had a buck—they'd just smell it," recalled Nevelson. When the time came for Rivera and Kahlo to return to Mexico, Nevelson and several other friends raised the money for tickets. Afraid the artists would give these away, too, the friends then "took them bodily onto the boat and saw that they left." Rivera, observed Nevelson with amused understatement, "had a great generosity."

Marjorie Eaton left New York soon afterward, and Nevelson suddenly felt lonely. To fill the hours when she was not drawing, sculpting, or taking classes, she began to study dance. Her instructor, Ellen Kearns, taught a new form of modern dance called *eurythmics*. Eurythmics, which Nevelson defined as "inner rhythm," is the art of interpreting the rhythm of a musical composition through movements of the body.

Nevelson, already a great admirer of such modern-dance pioneers as Martha Graham and Isadora Duncan, was wild with enthusiasm for Kearns and her method of dancing. "I became aware of every fiber [of my body]," she said, "and it freed me." She studied with Kearns for more than 20 years, practicing techniques that, she said later, helped her maintain her extraordinary productive energies well into her eighties.

Eager to share her discovery, Nevelson persuaded her sister Lillian to join her at Kearns's studio. Lillian, now married to New York artist Benjamin Mildwoff, had taken an apartment near Nevelson's Greenwich Village studio. At the Mildwoffs', Nevelson met Chaim Gross, a young sculptor whose cubistic clay figures had been exhibited at several prominent New York art galleries. Nevelson began to attend Gross's sculpture classes, where she worked in clay from live models. Impressed with her gifts, Gross prophesied that she would one day be known as a great sculptor.

He was right, but Nevelson's fame was still far in the future. The 1930s were hard years for artists, as they were for most Americans. The Great Depression, which followed the stock market crash of 1929, shook the nation's economy to its roots. Thousands of businesses failed, bankruptcies sky-

Martha Graham, *one of the modern dancers Nevelson most admired, strikes a characteristic pose in the 1940s. "For me," said Graham, "dance is life."*

rocketed, and millions of citizens—fully one-quarter of the labor force—were unemployed. In a time when few people could afford anything but the bare necessities of life, art became a luxury, and artists an endangered species.

Franklin D. Roosevelt, elected president in 1932, believed that the federal government was responsible for assisting needy citizens. Declaring a "New Deal" for America, he set up a series of programs designed to turn the economy around. One of them, the Works

47

President Franklin D. Roosevelt, seen greeting admirers in 1934, established a program that provided jobs for artists during the Great Depression of the 1930s.

Progress Administration (WPA), sponsored public-works projects that provided employment for thousands of people. The WPA concentrated on employing semiskilled and unskilled workers to build such projects as schools, roads, and dams, but it also offered a wide range of programs for unemployed professionals and artists.

The Federal Arts Project, a WPA sub-agency, paid artists to paint murals, create sculptures, and produce other artworks for public display. It also offered teaching jobs for artists. Started in 1935, the program kept hundreds of American artists from financial ruin.

Because she still had a little money, Nevelson was hesitant about joining the WPA at first. But times were getting worse. "In the toughest economic days," she recalled later, "I didn't have the price [5 cents on the subway] to go uptown." In 1935 she took a WPA job, teaching mural painting at the Flatbush Boys' Club in Brooklyn. Always rather suspicious of formal art instruction, she doubted that she would be a good teacher. But she waded in, encouraging her pupils to express their own feelings with paints and brushes. The boys responded enthusiastically to her unconventional approach, producing unexpected and often striking paintings that delighted her. In the end, she called her experience as an art instructor "a great adventure."

While she was teaching at the boys' club, Nevelson attended free WPA workshops where she learned how to cast statues in plaster and bronze and how to apply a *patina* (finish) to them. She was deeply grateful to the WPA, which she credited with saving not only her own career but also those of such great 20th-century artists as Willem de Kooning, Franz Kline, Mark Rothko, and Arshile Gorky. "Without that project," she said later, "I question whether the de Koonings and the Gorkys and the Klines and the Rothkos would have survived."

During the 1930s, Nevelson continued to develop her own talents. In one experiment, she painted some of her sculptures. "I was really searching for form," she said later. "I painted each plane [surface] a different primary color so that the form would be as clear a line as architecture." She started to exhibit her work at group shows, and it began to attract attention. In 1936 she showed five wooden sculptures at a Greenwich Village art gallery.

The pieces were, said a critic for the *New York Times*, "unlike anything we've seen before.... They are coated with multicolored paints. For example, one arm of a figure is painted blue and the other yellow. Or one-half of her chest is one color and the other half

Painters employed by the Works Progress Administration (WPA) decorate a New York City theater marquee in 1936. Nevelson was one of many artists who worked for the WPA.

another.... Colored sculpture is far from a new thing.... But Miss Nevelson uses color as it never has been used before. She applies it abstractly, so to speak."

Nevelson was encouraged by such public recognition, but she was not pleased by the attitude of some of her male colleagues. "The men did not really include me as an artist at all," she later told writer Roy Bogartz. "I was a good chick ... but I wasn't on their level." She also discussed the question of sexism with her friend and biographer, Diana MacKown.

"No one has a monopoly on creativity," she said. "I never recognized that whoever created humans gave a brain only to one sex or the other." She added that most women of the time were "taught to look pretty and throw little handkerchiefs around but never to show that they had what it takes. Well, I didn't recognize that and I never never played that role. If you play that role, you don't build an empire."

And an empire, she might have added, was exactly what she intended to build. Meanwhile, she continued to work and, as she put it, "to have fun." Talking to MacKown, she was candid about her life in this period. "I always used to dress with a flair," she said. "And I liked to swear and I liked to drink and have romances.... I was very sure of what I was doing. I believed in myself and I was utterly sat-

Nevelson sculpted Two Figures *(above) in 1933. "I couldn't afford bronze," she said later, "so I used Tattistone (a blend of marble dust and glue)."*

isfied with what I believed in. I wasn't going to let a soul on earth judge my life."

Nevelson's spirits in the 1930s swung between confident euphoria and periods of profound melancholy. She connected her periods of gloom with her work. "You know, when you're pregnant, there are the physical pains of nature," she observed in *Dawns + Dusks*. "But if labor pain is for physical birth, then there is a psychic pain . . .

for [artistic] creation. Through the periods of creation over the years I have had these deep psychic depressions. . . . I certainly entertained suicide. But I had this child and I was a parent and I just couldn't let anyone down."

In the autumn of 1936, Mike Nevelson came to New York City to live with his mother while he finished high school. He graduated in 1940 and soon afterward joined the merchant marine.

His departure shook Nevelson deeply. She had lived apart from him through most of his upbringing, justifying her absence by her need to practice her art. But she was now over 40, and she had achieved no significant success to balance her separation from her child. The WPA art program had ended in 1939, leaving her in financial as well as emotional distress. "I was so desperate," she later told MacKown, "that I decided that I had to have a show or I was going to cut my throat."

At this point, in the summer of 1941, a wealthy cousin of Nevelson's arrived in New York for a visit. He took her out for an elegant dinner and, traveling by chauffeured limousine, to an expensive Long Island resort for the weekend. "I suddenly realized that while I was having trouble sustaining myself," she later told biographer Arnold Glimcher, "he had spent a thousand dollars in two days." The time had come, she decided, to make some serious changes in her life.

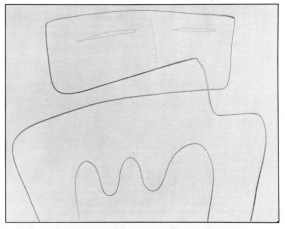

This untitled pencil drawing of a female figure, made in 1930, is now part of the Nevelson collection at New York City's Whitney Museum of American Art.

After lunching at Manhattan's posh Plaza Hotel, Nevelson said good-bye to her cousin. Then, she recalled, "I said to myself, what's the best gallery in New York?" Deciding it was Karl Nierendorf's 57th Street showroom, she marched over to 57th Street. "Well, I'm going in there," she thought, "and if I don't get a show, I'll shoot him."

Nevelson's 1946 oil painting, Self-Portrait, *bears little physical resemblance to the artist, whom most observers described as "beautiful."*

FIVE

"Geometry and Magic"

Art dealer Karl Nierendorf represented some of the era's most important artists, including Pablo Picasso and Paul Klee. When a total stranger stalked into his prestigious Manhattan gallery and demanded that he exhibit her sculpture, Nierendorf was astonished. "But I don't know your work!" he exclaimed. "Well," responded Louise Nevelson cheerfully, "you can come and see my work."

Intrigued, Nierendorf decided to have a look. The next day, he showed up at Nevelson's studio, where she had stored the sculptures she had made under the WPA art program. Nierendorf looked over the pieces and made a quick decision. "You can have a show in three weeks," he said. It would be Nevelson's first one-woman show. A splendid piece of luck? Not the way she looked at it.

"I think we create our lives. I'm not going to accept words like *luck* and *break*, none of it," she said in *Dawns + Dusks*. "I wouldn't permit it. I don't want breaks. I don't want the outside to superimpose. In my structural mind, I couldn't afford it."

However Nevelson looked at it, Nierendorf's offer was unusual for several reasons. First, his gallery was one of the most important in the nation; second, exhibits were normally booked a year in advance; finally, he had never shown the work of a woman artist or of an American. World War II, which had been raging in Europe for two years, had driven large numbers of Europeans to the United States. Many of these refugees, artists in particular, had settled in New York, which was now flooded with European paintings and sculpture. A large number of galleries,

Bombed by Japanese planes on December 7, 1941, U.S. ships burn at Pearl Harbor, Hawaii. The surprise attack brought the United States into World War II.

Nierendorf's included, were exhibiting only European artists.

With only a few weeks to prepare for her show, Nevelson frantically set about cleaning and repainting a selection of plaster sculptures from her WPA group. The Nierendorf exhibition could be a turning point: Good reviews would establish her in the art world; good sales would provide desperately needed income. The show, which opened on September 22, 1941, did receive encouraging notices.

"Modern indeed are the forms and rhythms employed by Louise Nevelson," said the critic for the *New York Times*. "Miss Nevelson has originality and . . . has made an interesting start." The *New York Herald Tribune* noted that her work contained "wit and a feeling of the primitive." Another reviewer commended Nevelson's "zestful interest in movement," calling her work "well off the beaten track" and "cleverly done."

Nevelson was pleased by the positive tone of these reviews, but one notice made her furious. Writing for *Cue* magazine, an anonymous critic wrote: "We learned the artist is a woman, in time to check our enthusiasm. Had it been otherwise, we might have hailed these sculptural expressions. . . . I suspect that the artist is clowning." To an artist who had struggled to free herself from sexual stereotyping, such patronizing words were especially painful.

More painful still was the outcome of the show: Not a single piece was sold. Nierendorf, by now a firm believer in Nevelson's future, was willing to lend her money, but her spirit had received a crushing blow. When the show closed, she went home to her large, drafty studio. She described the scene in *Dawns + Dusks*: "It was cold and I was miserable and I just lay in bed. And I saw *darkness* for weeks. It never dawned on me that I could come out of it, but you heal.... All of a sudden I saw a crack of light ... then all of a sudden I saw another crack of light. And I recognized that there was no darkness, that in darkness there'll always be light."

But there was more darkness to come. On December 7, 1941, Japanese bombers attacked the U.S. fleet at Pearl Harbor, Hawaii, and the United States entered World War II. Merchant marine seaman Mike Nevelson was now involved in dangerous supply missions throughout the world. Like millions of other Americans, Louise Nevelson anxiously waited for mail from overseas, which often took months to reach the United States. And she worried not only about her son but also about her mother, whose health had been deteriorating steadily.

Nevelson coped with her personal concerns by plunging back into her

Bicycle Wheel, *French artist Marcel Duchamp's aptly titled 1913 construction, is among the most celebrated works produced by the dada movement.*

work, preparing for her next exhibit at Nierendorf's gallery. "I didn't make sculpture to share my experience," she later said of this period. "I was doing it for myself. I did it because I knew I was in a spot, and I had to move out of it to survive." At this point, she began to experiment with "found objects," making sculptures from odd bits of wood. "Anywhere I found wood, I took it home and started working with it," she recalled later. "It might be on the

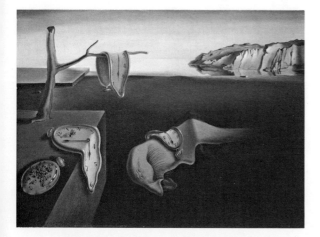

Salvador Dali's 1931 painting, The Persistence of Memory—*often called "The Limp Watches"—is among the surrealist movement's best-known works.*

streets, it might be from furniture factories. . . . It didn't really matter."

Like the first, Nevelson's second exhibit produced cordial reviews but no sales. It did, however, produce a rewarding new relationship for Nevelson. One of her friends arrived at the opening with Ralph Rosenborg, a 29-year-old artist who specialized in watercolor paintings of nature. He and Nevelson, then 42, were instantly attracted to each other. As she crisply told MacKown, "I met Ralph and he took me home to East 10th Street. So Ralph never left. . . ."

Nevelson had acquired many admirers since her separation from her husband, but most of her love affairs had been brief. Her meeting with Rosenborg marked the start of a long-lasting romantic relationship. She admired his work ("No one on earth has the touch of Ralph Rosenborg," she said), and he regarded her as a genius. Like her, he was enthusiastic about using wood as an art material, and he had nothing but praise for the sculptures she had started making with scraps of lumber and wooden furniture.

Soon after she met Rosenborg, Nevelson had an experience she called a "landmark in my own life." Out walking one stormy winter day, she spotted a patch of yellow in the swirling snowflakes. It was *so* yellow, she recalled, that it made everything else around it seem to vanish. The patch of color turned out to be a shoeshine box under the arm of an old man. Nevelson chased him down the street. When he stopped, she said, "You have a beautiful shoeshine box." She offered to buy it but he refused. Instead, he told her to meet him the following Monday. "I'll show you," he said, "the most beautiful shoeshine box in the world."

When Nevelson next met the old man, he proudly displayed his home-made shoeshine stand, a chair festooned with beads, bells, buckles, doorknobs, old costume jewelry, ribbons, and flowers. "I never saw anything like it," she recalled later. Dazzled by what she called a "superbly elegant work of art" and "the essence of Surrealism," she said, "Would you permit me to take this to the Museum of Modern Art?" The old man, probably

Paintings and statues, some by Nevelson and some by artists she admired, dominate the living room of the sculptor's house on Manhattan's East 30th Street.

Nevelson designed this 24-inch-high terra cotta sculpture, one of the Moving-Static-Moving figures she made in the 1940s, to change shape at the beholder's touch.

completely bemused by this human whirlwind, agreed. Nevelson called a friend at the museum, whisked the man and his chair into a truck, and took them uptown. Also impressed by the "throne with feet," museum officials set it up in the lobby as a Christmas exhibit.

After the incident, Karl Nierendorf confronted the sculptor. "Nevelson, what made you go to the museum? Nobody on earth would do that," he said. She blithely replied, "Where am I supposed to go with it?"

When Nevelson called the shoeshine stand "the essence of Surrealism," she was referring to the latest European art movement to take root in America. Although the work of many important artists, including Nevelson, would continue to show the imprint of cubism, its era was virtually over. It had been supplanted by surrealism, a style of art and literature that originated in Paris in the 1920s.

Surrealism had emerged from a post–World War I movement known as dada. Disillusioned with a society that glorified war, the dadaists attacked traditional values with a kind of anti-art, using nonsense as their principal weapon. The name of the movement, in fact, had been chosen at random from a French dictonary, and translated as "hobbyhorse." Prominent among the dadaists was Jean Arp, who specialized in torn-paper constructions. Another was Marcel Duchamp, a painter and sculptor who invented "readymades"—artworks that consisted of such items as bicycle wheels or bottle racks.

By the 1920s, dada, inherently self-critical, had reached its limits as a movement. Many dadaist artists moved on to surrealism, which sought to express the subconscious mind by depicting objects and events as they are seen in dreams. The surrealists believed that the blending of dream states with ordinary reality would produce *surréalité* (superreality), a new, perfected kind of reality. Best known of this group is Salvador Dali, the Spanish artist whose exquisitely detailed oil paintings often depict dream landscapes. Among Dali's most popular works is his "limp watch" painting, a 1931 canvas formally titled *The Persistence of Memory*.

Like all artists, Nevelson was influenced by everything she experienced; anything she saw, heard, smelled, or touched might play a part in her creative process. Her work in the 1940s, created in an atmosphere dominated by surrealism, inevitably reflected elements of that movement. For her third one-woman show, held at Manhattan's Norlyst Gallery in 1943, she created an entire surrealistic environment. Entitled *The Circus—The Clown Is the Center of the World*, the work was an ambitious undertaking. It was divided into three sections: *The Menagerie*, *The Clowns*, and *Audience Figure*.

Within each section were wood, metal, and glass figures depicting circus performers, animals, and spectators. Some of the figures were illuminated with colored lights, and several were designed to move. In his book *Louise Nevelson* Arnold Glimcher quotes the sculptor as she reminisced about the *Circus*. "I had a group of figures, taller than I am, and I painted them white. One figure was weeping and on its head there was a gold piece of furniture for a hat. I broke up mirrors and drilled and attached them so that they became tears of different shapes.... I placed [the animals] on big round tree slices. Underneath the slice I attached furniture casters and a rope so that you could pull them and move the animals all over the place."

The *Circus* reflected both cubist and surrealist influences. Like the Cubists, Nevelson broke her figures into basic shapes that suggested movement and change. Like the surrealists, she placed her pieces in a dreamlike atmosphere that ignored realistic proportion and predictable connections. "This work I know was far-out for America at the time," Nevelson told Diana MacKown. "It was very revolutionary."

While she was feverishly working to complete *Circus*, Nevelson received shattering news: Her beloved mother was dead at the age of 63. Her death was not unexpected, but it hit her daughter hard. Minna Berliawsky's unshakable love and faith had been a cornerstone of Nevelson's existence, and Nevelson had adored her. Unable even to discuss her loss with friends, the artist did the only thing she could: She worked harder than ever, hoping to dull her pain by the act of creation.

The Circus opened to enthusiastic reviews from New York's art critics. Even *Cue* magazine, which had once been so patronizing, praised the new show and called Nevelson a "sculptor bursting with youth, energy, and a touch that brings all things to life." In terms of sales, however, it was the same old story: There were none. Nevelson was not philosophical about this display of public indifference.

"I was goddamn angry," she told MacKown later. "And I'm not talking about sweet little anger, I mean a great ANGER.... All my life, people have told me not to waste my energies on anger, but I kept anger, I tapped it and tapped it. Anger has given me great strength." When the show closed, Nevelson employed some of that anger: She dismantled the entire exhibit and set fire to it. Into the bonfire she also tossed about 200 oil paintings she had completed earlier. As a result of this furious act, very little of Nevelson's pre-1943 output exists today. Photographs of some of the destroyed pieces remain, however, enabling art historians to trace her development as an artist.

Nevelson had received a small inheritance from her mother, and she now decided to spend it on a house. She needed a place big enough to work in and to store the immense piles of wood scraps she had started to collect. Soon after the *Circus* exhibit and its fiery conclusion, her friend Ralph Rosenborg found her the perfect building, a four-story Manhattan brownstone on East 30th Street. Her new home boasted seven marble fireplaces, high ceilings, and a large enclosed backyard where she could work on her massive sculptures, but it needed major repairs.

"Ralph was marvelous," the sculptor later told MacKown. "He could do anything. If a ceiling had to be moved two inches or a wall extended . . . he would do it in a minute." Nevelson made the entire ground floor into a studio, then furnished the place to her own taste: "I bought three sets of furniture, garden furniture, glass tables, and placed them throughout the house, four stories," she recalled with satisfaction.

She took full advantage of the backyard, which she turned into a kind of environmental artwork. She hung pieces of sculpture around its walls and placed mirrors in the ground to reflect the sky. She even planted a little "garden" of kitchen implements, which she painted black. ("That's what you do with them," explained Nevelson, who was no cook.) She would live in the 30th Street house for the next 15 years, creating some of her most memorable works of art there.

American servicemen and civilians celebrate V-J Day—the end of World War II—in New York City's Times Square on August 16, 1945.

Nevelson had been living in her new house for two years when World War II ended. With the Allies' 1945 defeat of Japan and Nazi Germany, a new era of American prosperity and optimism began. To Nevelson, however, the late 1940s brought neither wealth nor good fortune. Her father died in 1946, once again leaving her grief stricken but silent, seeking respite from her sorrow by working. The following year, just as she was preparing for an exhibition at the Nierendorf Gallery, Karl Nierendorf died suddenly.

In many ways, Nierendorf's death was even more painful for Nevelson than her father's. From the beginning, Nierendorf had believed she would become a great artist, an opinion he often repeated to her and others. He had given her her first gallery exhibit and had bolstered her sometimes flagging spirits through years of incessant work and almost nonexistent sales. "I had always considered him my spiritual godfather," said Nevelson.

With Nierendorf's death, Nevelson lost not only a loyal friend but also a gallery in which to show her work. Deeply depressed, she did not even try to arrange for representation by a new gallery; she found it difficult to work at all. After months of despondency, she realized she was suffering from more than a sense of loss: She was very ill. In 1948, doctors discovered and removed a pelvic tumor. Fortunately, it proved nonmalignant, but the surgery left her too weak to work with the heavy materials and tools she had been using in her sculpture.

Deciding to try her hand at ceramics, she began to work at the Sculpture Center, a cooperative workshop for artists in Greenwich Village. During the next two years, she created several hundred *terra-cotta* (earthenware) figures, using a highly unconventional method. Instead of molding the clay into figures and then firing it (baking it in an oven), she cut shapes out of flat slabs of clay. She pressed bits of fabric onto the shapes to give them texture, then etched their surfaces with a knife.

After the pieces were fired, she connected them with *dowels* (thin rods) to form abstract figures. The dowels allowed a viewer to pivot the sections of the figures, thus altering their overall composition. She called these pieces *Moving-Static-Moving-Figures*.

One critic described Nevelson's terra-cotta sculpture as a "squat, blunt combination of child's toy and prehistoric monument." Indeed, Nevelson had always been fascinated by ancient artifacts and working with Mexican muralist Diego Rivera had piqued her

Frida Kahlo, Diego Rivera's wife, painted this self-portrait in 1940. Nevelson last saw Kahlo in 1950, three years before the Mexican artist's death.

interest in pre-Columbian art, works made in Central and South America before the arrival of Christopher Columbus in 1492. After seeing a pair of gigantic Mayan *steles* (primitive ceremonial columns decorated with carving) at New York City's Museum of Natural History, she yearned to visit Mexico, where she could examine such works in their original settings. In 1950, her sister Anita offered to go with her—and to pay all the expenses. Nevelson jumped at the chance.

Mexico was everything she had expected and more. In Mexico City, she and her sister visited Diego Rivera and Frida Kahlo, enjoying a happy reunion and admiring the couple's vast collection of pre-Columbian art. It was Nevelson's last encounter with her friends: Kahlo died three years later; her husband, in 1957. Nevelson found the architecture and museums of Mexico City "just overwhelming," and she was stunned by the ancient sculptures and pyramids she saw in the Yucatán peninsula, southwest of the capital.

"Yucatán was a world of forms that at once I felt was mine," she recalled in *Dawns + Dusks*. It was "a world where East and West met, a world of geometry and magic." She was awed by what she called "the sculpture, the power, and the organization" of the religious shrines built many centuries earlier. "In the past they would talk about primitive countries," she told Diana MacKown. "But when you see their

The remains of a 7th-century Mayan temple tower over Chichén Itzá in Mexico's Yucatán Peninsula. Nevelson was awed by the Yucatán's "world of forms."

sundials and the way everything was done, truly, *we* are the primitive country. . . . They were the sophisticates. According to my book, Mexico and its sculptures and pyramids is number one."

Fifty years old, Nevelson had been struggling for recognition as an artist for decades. She had experienced something of a slump during the last several years, weighed down by illness and the deaths of her parents and her friend Nierendorf. Now, blazing with energy after her Mexican travels, she was ready to open a new chapter of her creative life. Her work would reflect the mysteries of pre-Columbian art, the structural framework of cubism, and the theatrical explorations of surrealism, among other influences. But it would be uniquely her own.

Nevelson contemplates a section of First Personage, *the wooden sculpture featured in her 1957 show,* The Forest, *at the Grand Central Moderns Gallery.*

Building an Empire

By the early 1950s, the American art scene was dominated by Abstract Expressionism, a revolutionary movement led by Nevelson's former teacher, Hans Hofmann. The Abstract Expressionists, who were influenced both by the surrealists and by such Mexican social-protest artists as Rivera and David Siqueiros, applied paint to their canvases in an exuberant, apparently random manner. Prominent among the group were Jackson Pollock, Mark Rothko, and Helen Frankenthaler.

The Abstract Expressionists' images sometimes suggested objects found in the real world, but they were more often free-form expressions of the artists' private visions. Perhaps the best-known and most controversial of these artists was Pollock, an "action painter" who dripped and spattered enamel on huge canvases to create thick, glisten-

ing webs of color. Like other members of the movement, he considered the act of painting just as important as the finished painting itself.

With the emergence of the Abstract Expressionists came a parallel movement in American sculpture, also emphasizing the abstract rather than the realistic. The abstract sculptors of the 1950s, many of whom worked with welded steel, included scrap-metal artist David Smith and John Chamberlain, who specialized in sculptures made from crushed automobiles. Although Nevelson remained firmly outside these movements, they inevitably affected her outlook.

"We [artists] pool our energies with other creative people," she observed in *Dawns + Dusks*. "My work is bound to be related to that of others. . . . I don't mean you copy. But I think when you live in a hunk of time, you reflect a hunk of time.... I think [the Abstract Expressionists] are marvelous. I love their art, and I love their energy. Nevertheless I had to go my own way."

Although she was still without a regular gallery in the early 1950s, Nevelson worked constantly. She created numerous small ceramic and wood sculptures as well as a series of etchings. In etching, the artist uses a sharp tool to draw on a glass or metal plate that has been coated with acid-resistant paste. After the design is completed, the plate is bathed in acid, which eats into the lines made by the artist. The plate is then cleaned, coated

with ink, and pressed onto paper, imprinting it with the design.

Nevelson had tried her hand at etching a few years earlier, but she had disliked the medium because of the equipment involved. "There were so many tools to use," she told Arnold Glimcher, "that I wondered if I was learning to make etchings or to be a surgeon." In 1953, when she decided to try etching again, she did it her own way. For a tool, she used a can opener; for a pattern, a piece of lace. This time, she was delighted. "I thought, 'Oh, this is marvelous, it's so quick and direct,'" she recalled later. "And the feel of it, I loved it . . . because it gave me so much

Artist Jackson Pollock created One (Number 31, 1950) *(below), by pouring, sprinkling, and dripping oil paint and enamel onto a white canvas.*

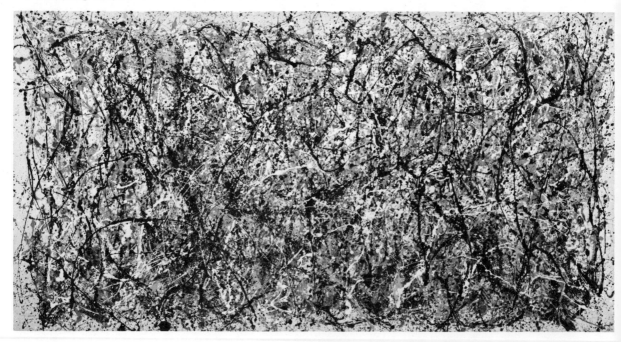

freedom to create." The results, seen in *Flower Queen* and other Nevelson prints of the 1950s, demonstrated a wholly original approach to the print-maker's art.

During this period, Nevelson joined several professional organizations, including the Federation of Modern Painters and Sculptors and the Sculptors Guild. But the group she enjoyed most was the Four O'Clock Forum, an informal artists' association that met at her 30th Street house on Sunday afternoons. Nevelson was happy to offer her home as a clubhouse for such contemporary giants as French artist Marcel Duchamp and Abstract Expressionists Mark Rothko and Willem de Kooning. "At the time," she recalled later, "things were interesting."

Nevelson had no one-woman shows between 1946 and 1955, but not for lack of trying. Determined to be noticed, she put her work into as many group exhibitions as she could. "I showed anywhere I was asked," she told Diana MacKown. "That's what I mean when I say I'm a yes woman. If they asked me, I showed. I didn't care where.... I remember a critic asked me, 'How the hell did you dare to show at so and such a place?' and I said, 'They asked me.' It was just as direct as that. My feeling is, show wherever you can." One fellow sculptor referred to her as "a little whirlwind of her own." Nevelson told friends: "I don't care whether it's prestigious or not. I'll flood

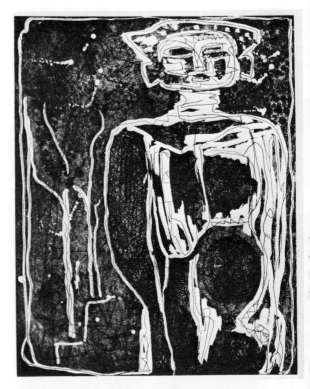

Nevelson etched Flower Queen *(above), one of her favorite two-dimensional works, in 1953. She said she enjoyed etching because it gave her the "freedom to create."*

the market with my work, so they'll know I'm here."

Finally, her strategy paid off. In 1955 she began a series of one-woman shows at the Grand Central Moderns, a new gallery in midtown Manhattan. The first exhibition, *Ancient Games and Ancient Places*, consisted of a group of wooden and ceramic sculptures, some of them with movable parts, some painted black and mounted on pedestals made from old packing crates.

Discussing such works as Black Majesty *(painted wood; 1955), Nevelson said, "It isn't black and it isn't wood. . . . [It is] an essence."*

Together, the pieces formed what Nevelson called "an environment." Because art is "so very living," she explained, "naturally you want all of life, so you make a total environment. . . . It's not only sculpture, it is a whole world."

Ancient Games was followed in 1956 by an exhibition entitled *Royal Voyage*.

Art critic Dore Ashton described it: "Kings and queens and things of the sea were symbolized in blocky, rough-hewn forms. . . . Characterized by a mixture of satire and fantasy, the pieces were united by the matte [non-shiny] black paint with which Nevelson drenched all her sculptures." *Royal Voyage* was the first of several

Nevelson, who called black "the most aristocratic color of all," prepares for a new sculpture by dipping a wood fragment in a can of black paint.

Nevelson shows in which all the figures were black. In *Dawns + Dusks*, she said, "When I fell in love with black, it contained all color. It wasn't a negation [cancellation] of color. It was an acceptance. Because black encompasses all colors. Black is the most aristocratic color of all." She saw black, she said, as the only color "that will give you the feeling of totality. Of peace. Of greatness. Of quietness. Of excitement."

After *Royal Voyage*, Nevelson started to work on her next show, which would be called *The Forest*. During this period, art critic Hilton Kramer visited the sculptor at her 30th Street home. "Nothing that one had seen in the galleries or museums or, indeed, in other artists' studios could have prepared one for . . . this strange house," he reported afterward. "Its interior seemed to have been stripped of everything—not only furniture, rugs, and the common comforts of daily living, but of many mundane [ordinary] necessities—that might divert attention from the sculptures that crowded every space, occupied every wall, and at once filled and bewildered the eye wherever it turned. . . . When one ascended the stairs, the walls of the stairwell enclosed the visitor in this same unremitting spectacle. Not even

Nevelson's artifact-crammed bathroom prompted a plaintive question from one art critic: "Where did one take a bath in this house?"

71

the bathrooms were exempted from its reach. Where, I wondered, did one take a bath in this house? For the bathtubs, too, were filled with sculpture."

The sculptures in *Ancient Games* and *Royal Voyage* reflected the city where Nevelson lived. For *The Forest*, her next exhibit, she drew on images from her childhood in Maine. The show's pieces represented a seaside village and the woods surrounding it. One of them, *First Personage* (now in the Brooklyn Museum), is among her best known works. Almost eight feet tall, this powerful sculpture is constructed from a massive slab of wood that suggests a human form. Adding to the figure's rather sinister appearance

is a vertical row of sharp spikes along one side. While she was working on it, Nevelson told Diana MacKown, she saw "a knot where the mouth was supposed to be, just a plain knot, and . . . all of a sudden I saw this knot, mouth, moving. And the whole thing was black by then and it frightened me."

Although Nevelson often worked herself to exhaustion, she still found time to socialize. She enjoyed giving parties, but entertaining was expensive. Aware of the sculptor's limited financial resources, a friend contributed a case of liquor for her 1957 Christmas party: It was a gift whose wrappings would prove far more useful than its contents. As Nevelson sur-

Among the sculptures in this Nevelson show is her celebrated First Personage, *an eight-foot-tall slab of wood backed by a spiked pole.*

veyed the wooden crate, its interior neatly partitioned to hold bottles, she suddenly saw a piece of sculpture. Excited by the idea, she filled each section with pieces of wood from the immense supply she kept on hand. She worked quickly. "I'm very fast," she said later. "I work at a certain speed and I like it, because it means you're not taking as much time to meditate. I like excitement. I don't like a meditative life."

Nevelson now acquired every box, crate, or other enclosure she could lay her hands on. She prowled Manhattan's streets, looking for discarded packing materials and carrying them back to her house. There she painted them black and filled them with such found objects as chair legs, broom handles, cabinet doors, even toilet seats. Her work space was soon overflowing with completed pieces, and she began to stack them, open sides facing outward, against the walls.

After she had covered one whole side of her studio with boxes, Nevelson realized that she had—almost accidentally—created a new work of art. Each of the boxes was an individual sculpture by itself; stacked side by side and one atop the other, they had become an environment, a place separate from everyday reality. In Nevelson's wall were elements of both the Abstract Expressionists' huge canvases and the intricately carved shrines built by the Indians of ancient Mexico.

Nevelson unveiled her wall, which she entitled *Sky Cathedral*, at the Grand Central Moderns Gallery in 1958. Part of a one-woman exhibit called *Moon Garden + One* (the "one," she explained, was the viewer), the wall startled the art community; it was, said Hilton Kramer, both "appalling and marvelous." For this show, Nevelson had transformed the gallery into a new world of mysterious black forms, a setting one critic called "a dark place of dreams and loneliness." She originally planned to leave the gallery unlighted, allowing viewers' eyes to adjust gradually to the darkness. Just before the show opened, however, she decided to bathe the sculptures in an eerie blue light, intensifying their mysterious quality.

"I composed the whole thing," said Nevelson in *Dawns + Dusks*. "It was not really for an audience, it was really for my visual eye. It was a feast—for myself." A gallery executive later reported that when Nevelson completed her arrangements, she "stripped herself of her work shirt, and radiant with joy . . . started to dance," as though she were thanking the forces that had "let her achieve her ultimate aim in life: Creation." What she had created, wrote Arnold Glimcher, was "a magic window that allowed the viewer to walk through into a private universe."

Moon Garden + One made Nevelson a star. New York City's Museum of Modern Art acquired the show's cen-

With 1958's Sky Cathedral *(above), Nevelson finally became a star. Critics called the work "marvelous"; to Nevelson, it was "a feast—for myself."*

terpiece, *Sky Cathedral*, and art collectors finally began to show interest in her work. In late 1958, the prestigious Martha Jackson Gallery offered her a contract: In return for the exclusive right to represent her, the gallery would guarantee her a minimum yearly income. The contract required her to supply the gallery with a specified number of pieces, but given her rapid rate of creation, this presented no problem. For the first time, Nevelson was financially secure.

But despite her newfound popularity, years of neglect by museum directors and the public had made her somewhat cynical. As a result, reported Arnold Glimcher, she was less than cordial to an important museum director who visited her after the *Moon Garden* show. He examined her work in silence, which she mistook for disapproval. Walking out to her backyard, she pointed to the city's skyline. "Look," she told the astonished director, "there's Grand Central Station and behind the Empire State Building is Penn Station—from these two places you can go anywhere in the world. Good day." And when another museum executive apologized for being slightly late for an appointment with her, she snapped, "What's ten minutes? Where were you ten years ago?"

When a New York developer decided to build a housing project on her block, Nevelson reluctantly sold her 30th Street home. In early 1959 she bought an old brick house on Spring Street in Little Italy, a neighborhood in the southern part of Manhattan largely populated by immigrants. She moved her vast stockpile of wood scraps into her new residence, then painted most of its interior walls her favorite color: black. Before long, the Spring Street house was as unmistakably Nevelsonian as its remarkable predecessor on 30th Street.

Nevelson had gained the respect of the New York art world. Still, she lacked one significant credential: a major museum exhibition. This gap was filled in 1959, when her friend Dorothy Miller, curator of the Museum of Modern Art, asked her to participate in the museum's *Sixteen Americans* show. In a burst of inspiration, Nevelson created a pure white world—*Dawn's Wedding Feast*—to balance the black world she had made earlier. The exhibition created a sensation and permanently established her as one of her era's most prominent artists.

Refusing to rest on her laurels, Nevelson continued to work nonstop. In 1961 she once again rocked the art world, this time with an environmental exhibit called *The Royal Tides*. In another sharp departure from her previous style, Nevelson sprayed all the pieces in *The Royal Tides* with gold paint. "Gold," explained the sculptor, "is a metal that reflects the great sun. And then when you put it on, it's an essence of a so-called reality in the

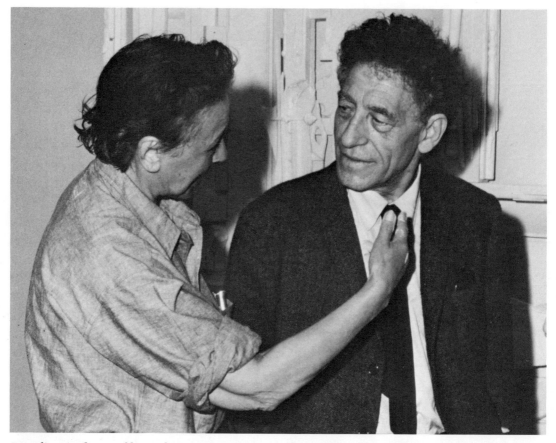

Standing in front of her white environment at the 1962 Venice Biennale, Nevelson congratulates the first-prize winner, Swiss sculptor Alberto Giacometti.

universe. Consequently I think why, in my particular case, gold came after the black and white is a natural. Really I was going back to the elements. Shadow, light, the sun, the moon."

Not everyone approved of Nevelson's gold period. Some art lovers, disappointed by her abandonment of the "mystery of black" and the "purity of white," called *The Royal Tides* "vulgar" and "a blatant display." Other viewers, however, were intrigued. Describing

the show, *Time* magazine reported, "Shallow honeycombs of orange-crate cabinetry are filled with carefully posed objects—chair legs, a broken wheel, a bowling pin, parts of a table pedestal, a banister, some toilet seats—all gleaming goldly." In their natural state, said the critic for *Art News*, these objects "could never have looked as august and glistening as they do now, transfixed by the Nevelson spell."

Nevelson was not without humor about her work. She answered one reporter's question about her new color by saying, "Well, I come from the Old Country....And they promised that the streets of America would be paved with gold." Responding to another query, she simply smiled and said, "Gold is money in the bank."

In 1962, she was invited to represent the United States at the Biennale Internazionale d'Arte, an important art exhibition and competition held every two years in Venice, Italy. Artists from all over the world dreamed of being selected for the Biennale, whose contestants in 1962 included such celebrated figures as the great Swiss sculptor Alberto Giacometti. "I was speechless," said Nevelson about receiving the invitation. She arrived in Venice on a Saturday, immediately taking part in a typical Nevelson scene.

Airline officials told her they had lost her luggage. But her exhibit opened on Monday, and she had no intention of making a grand entrance in her traveling clothes. When could she expect her bag? "Oh, maybe in a few days," said an official casually. Fixing the man with a direct stare, the 62-year-old artist said, "Now I'm getting married tomorrow and I've got to have my trousseau. My white wedding dress is in it!" No match for this determined "bride," the man hastily picked up a phone. "And sure enough," Nevelson recalled with a smile, "on Sunday the bag arrived."

For the show, she created three environments: one black, one white, and one gold. Her work was widely admired, but she lost the competition. "Giacometti, whom I got to know and adored, won the first prize in the exhibition that year, which was fine with me," she later told Diana MacKown. "Always the bridesmaid," she added cheerfully, "never the bride!"

Nevelson returned from Venice more self-assured than ever. After years of obscurity, she was now a celebrity, admired by the critics and public alike. Critic Dore Ashton referred to her work as "a total environment of which she is queen." She would spend the next two and a half decades conquering new territory for the empire she ruled.

Louise Nevelson visits her 37-year-old son, Mike, in 1959. Following in his mother's footsteps, Mike became a respected sculptor.

SEVEN

"The Busiest Artist in Town"

The early 1960s were good years for Nevelson. Her art was acclaimed all over the world, her son was emerging as a sculptor in his own right, and she had created a satisfying home in the city she loved.

Mike Nevelson, who turned 40 in 1962, was now married and starting a family in Connecticut. After World War II, he had returned to Rockland and once again taken up woodworking, the craft he had learned from his grandfather and uncle. Soon he was producing works that proved him both a fine cabinetmaker and an imaginative modern artist. The Farnsworth Library and Art Museum in Rockland had been exhibiting his sculpture since the early 1950s, and now he was represented by a well-known Manhattan art gallery.

Proud of her gifted son, Nevelson displayed his work prominently in her Spring Street house.

Visiting that house, recalled Arnold Glimcher in his Nevelson biography, was like taking a "trip to a natural phenomenon, like seeing the Grand Canyon." Filling every inch of floor and wall space in the five-story building were finished artworks and works in progress. Some rooms, said Glimcher, "were completely packed with boxes stacked densely to the ceiling, leaving only a narrow passage to walk through." When her work began to overflow her house, Nevelson rented a former pizza shop down the street; it, too, was soon filled with sculpture. Behind the pizzeria-studio was a courtyard where, Glimcher reported, the sculptor "often worked late into the night, the only illumination provided by the lighted tenement windows."

Nevelson occasionally displayed her own work in her living room, but most of the space was devoted to folk art: Tabletops, shelves, and even floors were crowded with primitive tools, African masks, pre-Columbian statues, Japanese chests, American Indian pottery, and carved wooden saints from Latin America. Presiding over this uniquely Nevelsonian clutter was the artist herself, usually wearing outfits that made their own distinctive statement. She had always enjoyed unusual clothes, particularly hats, and her costumes sometimes attracted as much attention as her artworks.

Time magazine once described her as "a cross between Catherine the Great and a bag lady." Viewing herself with candor and humor, she probably had no objection to the characterization. "I love to put things together," she told Diana MacKown. "Every time I put on clothes, I am creating a picture, a living picture for myself." Nevelson wore antique clothing years before it became fashionable. "I think I was the first person to wear a 16th-century Mandarin Chinese robe on top

Masks, pots, tools, and wood scraps fill the parlor of Nevelson's Manhattan home, described by one friend as "a natural phenomenon, like the Grand Canyon."

Dressed with her customary flair, Nevelson takes a telephone call at the Whitney Museum. "Every time I put on clothes," she once said, "I am creating a picture."

of a blue denim work shirt," she said. "For me clothes and presentation of self is a projection of the total personality.... Personally, I'm dramatic, it seems."

Dramatic was the right word for an outfit she wore to a museum opening in the 1960s. Arnold Glimcher described it: "A poncho fashioned of two deep purple silk Japanese tapestries, each embroidered with an enormous white crane, gray branches, and pink cherry blossoms. They were pinned together at the shoulder, sandwich-fashion, protecting a long, multiflounced black pleated Mexican skirt and a white, embroidered peasant blouse." Completing the costume was a boar's-tooth necklace, an enormous brooch made of black wood and solid gold, and an Egyptian-style turban fashioned from a bright turquoise table napkin.

The sculptor's "presentation of self" also included spectacular false eyelashes made of fur. "I don't feel dressed without my eyelashes," she told Mac-Kown. "I don't wear one pair; I glue several pairs together and then put them on. I like it and it's dramatic, so why not?" Her admirers agreed. Playwright Edward Albee (author of *Who's Afraid of Virginia Woolf?* and *A Delicate Balance*) called her "a bird of rare plumage." He wrote appreciatively of what he called "the Nevelson," a creature famed for "foot-long sable eyelashes framing the deep no-nonsense eyes, the coats of many colors, the splendid unexpected jewelry."

In 1962 "the Nevelson" signed a contract with Sidney Janis, a New York gallery owner who represented such important modern American artists as Jackson Pollock, Willem de Kooning, and Mark Rothko. The contract included no financial guarantee; if the gallery did not sell the sculptor's work, she would have no income. But Janis offered to lend Nevelson $20,000 to prepare for her first show, and she believed her association with him would increase her sales. She had made a serious mistake.

Nevelson's first (and last) show with Janis opened on New Year's Eve, 1962. The central works were three huge walls: *New Continent* (white), *Dawn* (gold), and *Totality Dark* (black). Like her earlier walls, these were assemblages of object-filled wooden boxes. This time, however, the boxes were not old wooden crates; Nevelson had them made to order by a carpenter. These walls were perfect, regular grids filled with such objects as rifle stocks, baseball bats, hat forms, and pieces of furniture. Critics would later list these pieces among her finest works, but at the time not one of them sold.

Nevelson decided to break off her business relationship with Janis. But because she had made nothing on the show, she could not repay the money he had lent her. And without the

*Producing prints at the Tamarind
Lithography Workshop in 1963, Nevelson
pulls a finished work from the inked
stone on which she has created a design.*

At this point she was invited to spend two months in Los Angeles, California, to make a series of experimental prints at the Tamarind Lithography Workshop. All her expenses would be paid by the Ford Foundation, a large nonprofit institution that often supported the arts. "I wouldn't ordinarily have gone . . . but I desperately needed to get out of town," she recalled later. It was an opportunity, observed Arnold Glimcher, that "saved Nevelson's life." At Tamarind, she concentrated on lithography, a printmaking process similar to etching. To make a lithograph, the artist draws on a flat, specially prepared stone, which is then bathed in ink and pressed on paper. As she had done with her etchings, Nevelson created patterns with pieces of lace and fabric.

Her energy and high spirits returning, Nevelson produced an imposing array of lithographs in just six weeks. The workshop director was amazed by both the quantity and the quality of these prints, whose collective worth she estimated at $150,000. "When I heard that, I was cured," Nevelson said later. "It wasn't that I had the money or was going to have it, it was just that it made everything bothering me seem . . . ludicrous."

When she returned to New York City in the spring of 1963, Nevelson signed up with Arnold Glimcher, director of the Pace Gallery and her future biographer. Between late 1963 and 1966,

money, Janis refused to return the three great walls to their creator. Nevelson was caught in a bind, suddenly deprived of the financial stability she had finally achieved after years of struggle. In order to cover her new debts, she was forced to borrow from friends. Now she had no gallery to represent her, no immediate sales prospects, no bank account. Even worse, art-world gossip suggested that she was finished, that her prominence had been only a passing fad and was now over. For the first time in years, she fell into a deep depression.

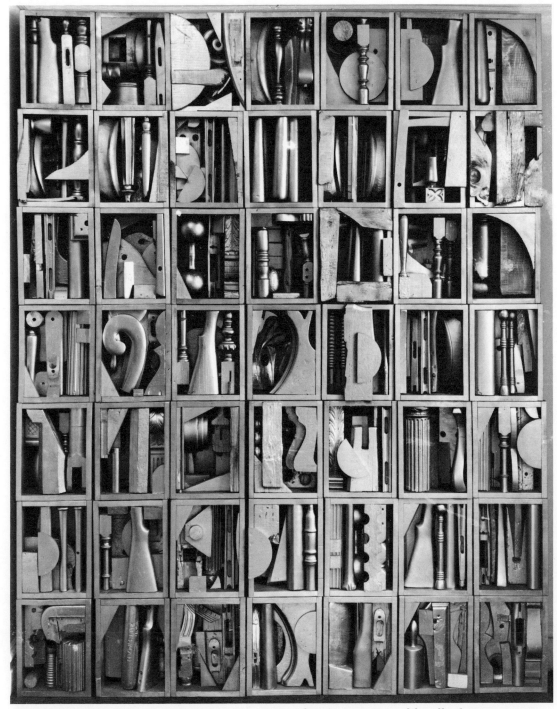

The finely crafted boxes comprising Dawn, Nevelson's massive gold wall of 1962, are filled with furniture sections, baseball bats, and rifle stocks.

she returned to one of her favorite mediums, black-painted wood. In 1964, for example, she completed *Homage 6,000,000* (the title referred to the Holocaust, the Nazi murder of six million Jews during World War II), a massive black wall whose subdivisions were filled with huge yarn spools and other large wooden objects. Glimcher called this work, which reflected both the past and the future, Nevelson's "successful attempt to reclaim her universe by reconstruction."

During this time, Nevelson also began to experiment with new materials. In *Self-Portrait*, for example, she used sheets of Plexiglas to cover the openings of an assemblage of stacked boxes. This lightweight, transparent plastic, she believed, created a sense of distance between the viewer and the objects in the boxes. And in *Silent Music I*, she covered the backs of the boxes with mirrors that reflected both the enclosed objects and the viewers themselves.

From mirrors and Plexiglas, Nevelson moved on to aluminum. She liked the idea of working in a material that would last; wood and plastics were durable, but metal was almost indestructible. As Glimcher put it, "Metal is attended by concepts of immortality to which Nevelson was not averse." She soon discovered that sculpting in aluminum would mean changing her working methods. When she used wood, she could hold the elements in place, "posing" them until she got the shape and design she was after. And wood was relatively cheap; if the artist made an imperfect piece, she could afford to toss it away and start again. Aluminum, on the other hand, was harder to maneuver and more expensive.

Deciding to make a large sculpture from black-enameled aluminum, Nevelson first constructed small-scale cardboard models of the components. Then she had the models duplicated in opaque (nontransparent) black Plexiglas, which would resemble enameled aluminum. After building one of her trademark walls with the Plexiglas units, she set it on a windowsill so she could study the way the changing daylight affected it. Once she was satisfied, she sent it to a *foundry* (a factory that manufactures castings from molten metal), where it was copied on a much larger scale in aluminum.

The finished piece, *Atmosphere and Environment I*, was huge: more than 12 feet wide, 6 feet high, and 4 feet deep. Unveiled in 1966 (and later acquired by the Museum of Modern Art), it marked Nevelson's first important use of metal. It also marked her first use of open-backed boxes, which made the scenery behind the sculpture part of the artwork itself. *Atmosphere and Environment I*, remarked Arnold Glimcher, "succeeded in packaging and enclosing the changeable qualities of landscape itself."

Nevelson and her friend and biographer, gallery director Arnold Glimcher, inspect a possible sculpture site in New York City.

By 1966, Nevelson's reputation—and her financial situation—had recovered completely. Her works were eagerly sought by collectors, and her shows at Pace were uniformly successful. Now, at the age of 67, she made a major change in the way she lived. First, she sold the art she had collected over the years: all the masks, statues, totems, pottery pieces, and Oriental chests. Then she scraped the black paint from the floors of her house and covered the walls with white paint. Next, she sold or threw away all her furniture, replacing it with steel lockers and cabinets and simple wooden tables and chairs. Soft chairs, she asserted, produced only "boring, comfortable conversations."

From that point forward, said Arnold Glimcher, going to Nevelson's house was "like visiting a monastery." The artist was delighted with the changes she had made. "I believe that the inheritance of ancestry and religion is a crime," she said firmly. "To be further hindered by possessions that I must take to the grave would be unthinkable."

But Nevelson's thoughts were far

A chest of drawers designed by Mike Nevelson stands in his mother's bedroom in 1971. Five years earlier Nevelson had cleared her house of most of its clutter.

from the grave. A few months after she redecorated her house, she selected works for a major show at New York City's Whitney Museum of American Art. The exhibition was a *retrospective* (a display of an artist's works from the current moment back to her or his beginnings). Nevelson was honored— the retrospective spotlighted her as one of America's most important artists—but she did not like the suggestion that it included *all* her work.

"We haven't even started yet," she said.

Nevelson herself designed the exhibit, which took up an entire floor of the Whitney. Included were early terra-cotta and plaster pieces, etchings, small wood and metal sculptures, and such huge works as *Sky Cathedral*, on loan from New York's Museum of Modern Art. She transformed the exhibition space into a series of dramatically lit environments. Between two of the rooms, she constructed *Rain*

Forest, a collection of wooden columns, Plexiglas sheets, and suspended black moons that suggested a tropical jungle. Like most of Nevelson's environments, it existed only for the duration of the show; afterward it was dismantled and sold as separate pieces.

"That show was very meaningful to me," recalled the artist. But it contained one element she disliked: the terra-cotta figures she had made in the 1930s and 1940s. She had been reluctant to include them, but the Whitney's director had insisted, asserting that without them the show would not trace her development as an artist. She was particularly unhappy about exhibiting *Earth Figure*, a large statue of a running woman, which she had never liked. Just before the show opened, she and Arnold Glimcher made a final check on arrangements.

They were alone in the gallery. Nevelson asked Glimcher to move the *Earth Figure* across the room so she could see if it looked any better there. Then, when he was halfway across the room, she shouted, "Drop it!" The sculpture shattered on the floor. Nevelson telephoned the museum director to apologize for the "accident," which was, she said, entirely her own fault. Glimcher wrote, "She was now satisfied with the exhibition; she had edited out the weakest piece."

Included in the Whitney retrospective was a new kind of Nevelson work: a sculpture made completely of Plexiglas. This piece, *Ice Palace I*, was the first of 13 transparent, geometric sculptures that Nevelson would create during the next 2 years. The Plexiglas works intrigued viewers, who praised their "cool, detached glamour." In them, said a *New York Times* art critic, "structure is no longer designed to 'contain' the image; increasingly, it *is* the image."

Nevelson had succeeded with wood, with aluminum, with Plexiglas. "So then I naturally wanted the next step," she recalled in *Dawns + Dusks*. "I had been through the shadow. I had been through the enclosure of light and reflection. And now I was ready to take away the enclosures and come out into the open." She was, in other words, ready to face a new challenge: monumental outdoor sculpture. Her new material would be cor-ten steel, an *alloy* (mixture) of metals that develops a rust-colored surface when it is exposed to air. Nevelson, who called cor-ten "a blessing," said she was soon using the tough steel as though it were "ribbon made out of satin."

Over the years, Nevelson had been offered many commissions, but she had always turned them down, fearing she would be "fenced in" by a work-to-order job. But she was so excited about cor-ten that when Princeton University offered her a sculpture commission in 1969, she accepted it. Entitled *Atmosphere and Environment X*,

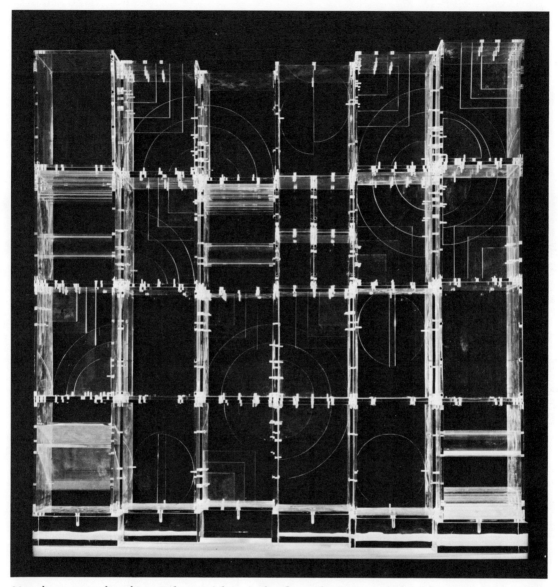

Nevelson completed Ice Palace I *(above), the first of a series of Plexiglas sculptures, in 1967. Art critics called her transparent pieces "glamorous."*

the 16-foot-tall Princeton piece consists of Nevelson's familiar stacked boxes, some of them open, some closed, some of them filled, others empty. Arnold Glimcher, who described the work as "the frozen promise of a building in its skeletal stage of construction," noted that "as the sun changes, the boxes cast angular shadows, [creating] a honeycomb of light and dark."

Two years after she completed the Princeton sculpture, Nevelson spotted a pile of aluminum scraps during a visit to a foundry. Quickly seeing their possibilities, she turned the scraps into 10 plantlike sculptures, which she grouped together and called *Seventh Decade Garden*. (At 71, she was now in her eighth decade, but no one disputed the arithmetic of the "Queen.") The garden pieces brought instant critical praise when they were displayed at the Pace Gallery.

Writing in the *New York Times*, John Canaday jokingly complained that the sculptor was making it difficult for art lovers to keep up with her. "For several years now, from show to show, she has implicitly capped off her career with a final demonstration of her powers of invention," he said. "But each following year she comes up with something new."

Canaday had understated the case. Starting in 1972, Nevelson made a series of 37 "dream houses," fanciful black wood structures with roofs, windows, and doors that opened into shadowy black interiors. Also in 1972, she created *Night Presence IV*, a 22-foot-high cor-ten steel sculpture that she presented to New York City for Christmas. "I thought it fitting that I should give something of myself," she said, "to this wonderful city where I

First Lady Betty Ford joins Nevelson in front of Bicentennial Dawn, *the sculptor's tribute to the United States on its 200th birthday in 1976.*

have lived and worked and created for 50 years." (The work remains in place on Park Avenue and 92nd Street in Manhattan.) In 1974 she began to work on *Bicentennial Dawn*, a sculpture commissioned for the nation's 200th-birthday celebration in 1976.

Installed in the cavernous lobby of Philadelphia's federal courthouse, *Bicentennial Dawn* was an immense, three-section work, constructed entirely of white-painted wood. Unlike such earlier works as 1959's *Dawn's* *Wedding Feast*, the bicentennial sculpture contained no found elements; it was composed entirely of forms created by Nevelson. Art critics outdid one another in heaping praise on the new piece. "I know of no single public

A reflecting pool surrounds Nevelson's Atmosphere and Environment XIII, *a 14-foot-tall cor-ten sculpture installed in Scottsdale, Arizona, in 1972.*

rhythms as lyrical as they are complex."

When the Pace Gallery unveiled a new Nevelson exhibit in February 1976, Hilton Kramer of the *New York Times* applauded the show's "enchanting constructions" and their "astounding" creator. Nevelson, he said, "is one of the busiest artists in town—indeed, one of the busiest artists in many a town." He mentioned her latest commissions—not only *Bicentennial Dawn* in Philadelphia, but huge outdoor pieces in Cambridge, Massachusetts; Wichita, Kansas; Binghamton, New York; and Scottsdale, Arizona. "And this by no means exhausts the list of recent and current projects," he said. "It is all rather amazing, and one could easily understand if, in the face of these commissions, the artist had chosen to take a temporary furlough [vacation] from the normal round of studio work. But the idea of such a furlough is clearly alien to an artist of Mrs. Nevelson's formidable energy."

Kramer was right. At the age of 77, Louise Nevelson was still the "workhorse" she had always been. "I've never had a day when I didn't want to work," she recalled in *Dawns + Dusks*. "If I don't work, I'm not breathing. I have to breathe to live."

sculpture anywhere in the country more beautiful than this newest Nevelson," wrote Emily Genauer in the *New York Post*. "For all its monumentality, *Bicentennial Dawn* is shaped with unusual delicacy...to make

93

Headscarf and long eyelashes in place, Nevelson supervises the 1979 installation of a 15-ton steel sculpture, Frozen Laces, *near Manhattan's Central Park.*

EIGHT

"America's Greatest Living Sculptor"

Indoors and outdoors, from New York to San Francisco, the whole country seems on its way to becoming one big Nevelson sculpture garden," wrote Hilton Kramer in the *New York Times*. "Her photographic image, too, stares at us everywhere we turn," he added. "It is now as familiar as Picasso's." Indeed, Nevelson's wildly unconventional personal style had become almost as celebrated as her art. In 1977, it even earned her a spot on the annual list of America's best-dressed women. Offering its own explanation for this phenomenon, *Time* magazine said, "There was nowhere else to put her and no way to ignore her."

Nevelson's hard years were now behind her. Now, too, her guilt about neglecting her only child seemed a distant memory. "My son? I'm glad you asked me," she told a *New York Post* reporter in late 1977. "He's Mike Nevelson and he's 55 and he lives in Fairfield, Connecticut, a sculptor working all the time." She was, she added proudly, a grandmother with "one great-grandchild and another on the way." Mother and son kept in touch quite often. Biographer Natalie Bober quotes an amused friend who had overheard a telephone conversation between the two. "Yes, Mother," the middle-aged sculptor had said. "Yes, I've eaten. I *had* lunch. I *have* eaten, Mother."

In 1977, Nevelson was the star of two major art events in New York City. The first occurred in the Chapel of the Good Shepherd at St. Peter's Lutheran

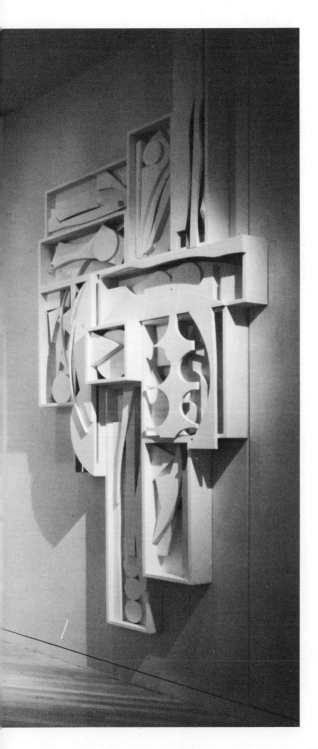

Nevelson's abstract religious symbols adorn the walls of the Chapel of the Good Shepherd, part of St. Peter's Lutheran Church in New York City.

Church, a house of worship tucked into a brand-new Manhattan skyscraper. Commissioned to design the interior of the tiny, odd-shaped chapel, Nevelson had created a dazzling white environment. On each of its five walls, she had placed sculptures representing saints and religious symbols. She had even designed the ministers' white robes and the chapel's centerpiece, a sparkling, gold-and-white cross.

The *New York Times* called the chapel "one of the great successes of [Nevelson's] career," one that demonstrated "the powers of adaptation that some artists can carry into old age." When the chapel opened, a reporter asked the pastor why a Russian-born Jewish artist had been chosen to design an American Protestant church. The clergyman's answer was simple. "Because," he said, "she's the greatest living American sculptor."

Nevelson's second 1977 triumph took place in the Pace Gallery. Here, the spotlight was on *Mrs. N's Palace*, the largest sculpture Nevelson (whose neighbors called her Mrs. N) had ever made. The palace was a houselike structure set on a huge panel of black mirrored glass. Viewers could actually enter the building, whose walls were encrusted with what one reviewer called "elegantly composed sculpture." Guarding the door were the massive, shadowy forms of a king and queen, figures Nevelson had made years earlier.

Mrs. N's Palace awed critics and public alike. "This is no mere haunted house," said *Time* magazine. "Collection, repetition, unification: these are the elements of Nevelson's poetic but wholly sculptural sensibility, and this time they have produced a masterpiece." Hilton Kramer wrote, "If one had to choose one work that contains the essence of [Nevelson's] achievement, this would be it, and is clearly intended to be it. It is an experience not to be missed." *Art News* called the work "a palace for the child in all of us."

While the piece was still on exhibit, a West German museum offered to buy it for $1 million. Nevelson—who had once fretted about her lack of money and the world's lack of interest in her work—quickly turned the offer down. She wanted the *Palace* to stay in New York City. (Eight years later, she would donate it to New York City's Metropolitan Museum of Art.)

Nevelson had never made a secret of her love for her adopted hometown. "I have a feeling of New York City as if it were a person," she told Diana Mac-Kown. "The city and I have a lot in common." Returning her affection, the city named a park for her. In 1978, Legion Memorial Square, a triangular plot in Manhattan's downtown business district, was renamed Louise Nevelson Plaza. At the dedication ceremony, *Shadows and Flags*, a grouping of seven monumental Nevelson sculptures, was unveiled in the plaza. These sturdy freestanding pieces, constructed of black welded steel, formed a massive but graceful presence amid Wall Street's somber towers.

As Nevelson's 80th birthday approached, she was the subject of national attention. Newspapers, magazines, and television news shows ran countless stories and programs about her, and museums across the country held retrospective exhibitions. She was especially touched by one of these shows: It was staged by the Farnsworth Library and Art Museum in Rockland, Maine. In 1979, Nevelson returned to Rockland in glory, happy to be lionized by the town that had once made her feel so isolated. Joining her in Rockland were her brother, Nate, and her sister Anita, but missing was her sister Lillian, who had died two years earlier. Nevelson had grieved for Lillian, but she was untroubled by the prospect of her own death.

"I have never feared not living, never, not even in youth," she said to Mac-Kown. But she did sometimes grumble about her advancing years. "To confront 80 is a problem," she told *Art News* in 1979. Then, ignoring her own statement, she continued to work at her usual breakneck pace. In 1979 she constructed *The Bendix Trilogy*, three

Mrs. N's Palace, *Nevelson's spectacular 1977 sculpture, was hailed by one critic as "an experience not to be missed." Another simply called it "a masterpiece."*

Erected in 1978, a street sign demonstrates New York City's affection for Nevelson. The sculptor said she thought of New York "as if it were a person."

large cor-ten steel structures, which were installed in Southfield, Michigan. In 1980 she created a 30-foot-tall steel sculpture for Kansas City, Missouri; later that year she produced a similar work for the University of Iowa.

In 1982, Nevelson received a present few others might have appreciated: fragments of an old church organ. She quickly painted them black and turned them into a group of sculptures entitled *Cascades, Perpendiculars, Silence,*

Music. Reviving her old passion for delicate fabrics, in 1983 she created a series of monumental black steel sculptures called *Frozen Laces.*

Nevelson's nonstop activities ranged far beyond her workshop. On a local level, she campaigned for the preservation of landmark buildings in Little Italy, where she also helped establish a neighborhood youth center. She contributed to cancer research programs, worked for the nuclear-freeze movement, and supported groups that helped Jews emigrate from the Soviet Union. And, always an outspoken feminist, she strongly backed the women's movement, which she called "part of the general struggle for freedom today."

Working for a broad array of causes—and at the same time producing a steady stream of monumental art—might have exhausted a person half Nevelson's age, but she seemed to be tireless. In her ninth decade, she continued her high-profile social life, often attending glittering parties and gallery openings. But she never lost sight of her priorities—or her sense of humor. Interviewed by a *New York Post* reporter in 1984, she related a recent incident:

"One night I'm in chinchilla [her fur coat] going to this glamorous party at 68th and Madison and I see barrel staves sticking out from the street trash bin. Well, what. . . . am I going to do? I need these wonderful things. So I picked them out of the garbage can. A cop came by and stared like I was a nut." The episode, she said, ended peacefully: "I explained and he sort of understood."

By now, understanding—and appreciating—Nevelson had become something of a national pastime. In 1985 she became one of the first recipients of a new honor, the National Medal for the Arts. In the same year, she received an honorary degree from Harvard University, where her sculpture *Night Wall I* had just been installed. By 1987 her awards included the French Legion of Honor, the Medal of Freedom from the City of New York (honoring great Americans who had started as immigrants), the New York Governor's Art Award, and the Butler Medal for Life Achievement in American Art.

Showered with honors, known as "the grande dame of contemporary sculpture," Nevelson had become an institution. But she did not allow her success to change her way of life: In her late eighties she still rose at 6:30 in the morning to begin her day's work. Clearly, she had no intention of retiring. She explained her thinking to *New York Times* reporter Nan Robertson: "I have lived and I have been fulfilled. I recognized what I had, and I never sold it short. And I ain't through yet!"

In 1986, Nevelson opened an exhibit of her latest sculptures and collages—assemblages of plywood, scrap metal, electrical cord, and other found

New York City's financial towers form an imposing backdrop for Shadows and Flags, *the seven-part, black steel sculpture Nevelson constructed in 1978.*

objects—and once again surprised her audience. "Louise Nevelson is up to something new," wrote William Zimmer in the *New York Times*. "In her series of wood elements painted black, *Mirror Shadows*, her enclosing compartments are largely gone and the works are no longer rooted to the floor." Zimmer marveled at the continuing inventiveness of the 86-year-old artist; her display of "a new dynamism," he said, "wins one's admiration."

Writing in the *New Yorker* magazine in the spring of 1988, an old friend of Nevelson's recalled a visit to the artist a few months earlier. She had just returned from a trip to Ohio, where she had received the Butler Medal. "She was in tearing high spirits," said her friend. "Nothing would do but we climb with her to the roof of her house, on Spring Street, and admire the roses still in bloom in the helter-skelter garden she had fashioned there. . . . In her 89th year, Nevelson was, as usual, full of plans for the future."

Noting that the sculptor had achieved public success late in life, the *New Yorker* writer said that "she took care to diminish the significance of this fact by giving every sign, in the years and decades that followed, of intending to keep impertinent death at a distance for as long as she found it convenient to do so. . . . Her friends were inclined to believe that she was indeed capable of outwitting nature in

Welcoming his famous sister back to Rockland in 1979, Nathan Berliawsky jokingly suggests that she make a sculpture out of the old family fence.

almost every respect—certainly in respect to old age, if not to death."

But not even Nevelson could outwit nature forever. On April 17, 1988, her strong heart stopped at last, and she died peacefully at her Spring Street home. Tributes poured in from all over the world, hailing her as a towering figure—a great artist, an incomparable human being, a uniquely individualistic woman.

Nevelson had often said she intended to "build an empire," and that is exactly what she did. "She turned out to be one of those artists," said Hilton Kramer, "who changed the way we look at things." Nevelson, claimed another journalist, "left a legacy of stunning environmental art. Her . . . sculptures—made of shallow, cubistic boxes and filled with dark dreams and private passions—stand out as idio-

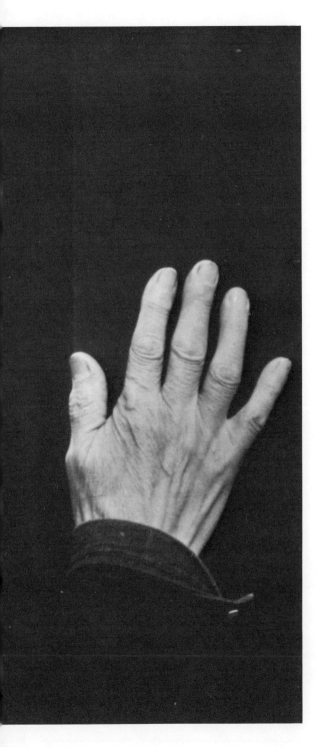

syncratic icons [highly personal images] of 20th-century art."

In eulogizing Nevelson, many writers noted that the artist and her work were indistinguishable, both of them "monumental and uncompromising." Her "art and persona," said playwright Edward Albee, were "perhaps more the same thing—in the very best of senses" than any other artist's. The playwright described her sculptures as "exquisite, powerful, remote, primordial, and always intellectually stimulating." Asked to describe her personality, he said, "For the clearest view of Nevelson, I point you to her work. She is there."

In *Dawns + Dusks*, Nevelson recalled an interviewer who asked her about reincarnation, the belief that after death, the soul returns to the earth in another body. "I don't believe in reincarnation," said the sculptor, "but let's assume that I'll accept the question."

"What would you like to come back as in your next life?" asked the interviewer.

Nevelson laughed. "Louise Nevelson," she said.

Nevelson's belief that "you can be anything you want to be," said one friend after the sculptor's death in 1988, was "the key to the freedom she achieved as woman as well as artist."

FURTHER READING

Barr, Alfred H. *Painting and Sculpture in the Museum of Modern Art 1929–1967*. New York: Museum of Modern Art, 1977.

Bober, Natalie S. *Breaking Tradition, The Story of Louise Nevelson*. New York: Atheneum, 1984.

Frank, Elizabeth. *Pollock*. New York: Abbeville Press, 1983.

Glimcher, Arnold. *Louise Nevelson*. New York: Dutton, 1976.

Goodman, Cynthia. *Hans Hofmann*. New York: Abbeville Press, 1986.

Lipman, Jean. *Nevelson's World*. New York: Hudson Hills, 1983.

Munro, Eleanor. *Originals: American Women Artists*. New York: Simon & Schuster, 1979.

Nevelson, Louise. *Louise Nevelson: Atmospheres and Environments*. New York: Crown, 1980.

———. *Nevelson: The Prints*. New York: Pace Gallery Publications, 1974.

———. *Nevelson: Wood Sculptures*. New York: Dutton, 1973.

———. *Sculptures in Black*. Chicago: Arts Club of Chicago, 1968.

Nevelson, Louise, and Diana MacKown. *Dawns + Dusks*. New York: Scribners, 1976.

Penrose, Roland. *Picasso*. London: Phaidon, 1971.

Schwartz, Constance. *Nevelson and O'Keeffe: Independents of the Twentieth Century*. Roslyn Harbor, NY: The Nassau County Museum of Fine Art, 1983.

Stodelle, Ernestine. *Deep Song, The Dance Story of Martha Graham*. New York: Macmillan (Schirmer Books), 1981.

Wilson, Laurie. *Louise Nevelson, Iconography and Sources*. New York and London: Garland Publishing, 1981.

CHRONOLOGY

September 23, 1899	Born Louise Berliawsky in Kiev, Russia
1905	Emigrates with her family to Rockland, Maine
1920	Marries shipowner Charles Nevelson; moves to New York City
1922	Gives birth to a son, Myron
1931	Separates from her husband; travels twice to Europe to study art
1935	Joins the WPA artist assistance program in New York City; begins sculpting
1941	Stages her first one-woman show (at Manhattan's Nierendorf Gallery)
1942–47	Continues yearly shows at the Nierendorf Gallery
1950–51	Travels to Mexico; returns to New York and begins sculpting in black-painted wood
1955	Begins a series of one-woman shows at Grand Central Moderns Gallery
1958	Receives critical acclaim for *Moon Garden + One*, exhibited at Grand Central Moderns
1959	Contributes her first white environment, *Dawn's Wedding Feast*, to the Museum of Modern Art's group show, *Sixteen Americans*
1962	Represents the United States in the sculpture section of the Venice Biennale
1967	Presents a major retrospective exhibition of her work at New York City's Whitney Museum of American Art
1969	Creates her first large-scale steel sculpture, installed at Princeton University
1971	Exhibits a group of freestanding metal sculptures, *Seventh Decade Garden*, at Pace Gallery
1976	Completes *Bicentennial Dawn*, a large three-part white-wood sculpture
1977	Creates a white environmental sculpture for the Chapel of the Good Shepherd at Saint Peter's Church in New York City
1978	Constructs *Shadows and Flags*, a group of huge steel sculptures for the newly named Louise Nevelson Plaza in downtown Manhattan
1985	Receives National Medal for the Arts
April 17, 1988	Dies in New York City

INDEX

INDEX

INDEX

PICTURE CREDITS

Michael Cain is a writer whose subjects have ranged from Baroque painters to American presidents. His fiction and nonfiction have appeared in various periodicals, including *California Quarterly* and *Wooster Review*. He has also written, directed, and edited film and video presentations. He currently resides in New York.

❖   ❖   ❖

Matina S. Horner is president of Radcliffe College and associate professor of psychology and social relations at Harvard University. She is best known for her studies of women's motivation, achievement, and personality development. Dr. Horner serves on several national boards and advisory councils, including those of the National Science Foundation, Time Inc., and the Women's Research and Education Institute. She earned her B. A. from Bryn Mawr College and Ph.D. from the University of Michigan, and holds honorary degrees from many colleges and universities, including Mount Holyoke, Smith, Tufts, and the University of Pennsylvania.